Computer Performance Measurement and Evaluation Methods: Analysis and Applications

ELSEVIER COMPUTER SCIENCE LIBRARY

Operating and Programming Systems Series   Peter J. Denning, *Editor*

1. *Halstead*
   A Laboratory Manual for
   Compiler and Operating System
   Implementation

Spirn
Program Behavior: Models and
Measurement (in prep.)

Programming Languages Series   Thomas E. Cheatham, *Editor*

1. *Heindel and Roberto*
   LANG-PAK—An Interactive
   Language Design System
2. *Wulf et al.*
   The Design of an Optimizing
   Compiler
3. *Maurer*
   The Programmer's Introduction to
   SNOBOL

Cleaveland and Uzgalis
Grammars for Programming
Languages (in prep.)
Hecht
Global Code Improvement (in prep.)

Theory of Computation Series   Patrick C. Fischer, *Editor*

1. *Borodin and Munro*
   The Computational Complexity of
   Algebraic and Numeric Problems

Computer Design and Architecture Series   Edward J. McCluskey, *Editor*

1. *Salisbury*
   Microprogrammable Computer
   Architectures
2. *Svobodova*
   Computer Performance
   Measurement and Evaluation
   Methods: Analysis and Application

Wakerly
Error-Detecting Codes, Self-
Checking Circuits and Applications
(in prep.)

Artificial Intelligence Series   Nils J. Nilsson, *Editor*

1. *Sussman*
   A Computer Model of Skill
   Acquisition

2. *Shortliffe*
   Computer-Based Medical
   Consultations: MYCIN

Computer Performance Measurement and Evaluation Methods: Analysis and Applications

Liba Svobodova
Massachusetts Institute of Technology

ELSEVIER
New York/Oxford/Amsterdam

AMERICAN ELSEVIER PUBLISHING COMPANY, INC.
52 Vanderbilt Avenue, New York, NY 10017

ELSEVIER SCIENTIFIC PUBLISHING COMPANY
335 Jan Van Galenstraat, P.O. Box 211
Amsterdam, The Netherlands

Library of Congress Cataloging in Publication Data

Svobodova, Liba.
Computer performance measurement and evaluation
methods : analysis and applications.

(Computer design and architecture series ; 2)
(Elsevier computer science library)
Includes bibliographies and index.
1. Electronic digital computers—Evaluation.
I. Title.
QA76.9.E94S94   001.6'4   76-18682
ISBN 0-444-00192-1
ISBN 0-444-00197-2 pbk.

Manufactured in the United States of America

To my parents

Contents

Preface

Analysis and evaluation of computer system performance has become an important and demanding field. Important because performance is one of the prime considerations in evaluating a computer system. Demanding because it requires a deep understanding of the inner system mechanisms, both hardware and software, knowledge of the processing requirements, understanding of the user's habits, adaptability to system changes and preferences, and the effects of poor performance on the user's productivity and well-being. As a result of demand for more powerful and flexible computing services and better performance per cost, computer systems have become increasingly complex, and system performance increasingly difficult to assess. Performance evaluation it not just determining whether or not a system meets certain objectives; it is also understanding if and how system performance can be improved. A computer system analyst must master a number of techniques to ascertain important factors and their effect on system performance. In the vast literature on computer performance and performance evaluation, only a few works discuss the relative utility of different techniques, their proper application and inter-relation. Thus, it is hard to acquire the needed information on applicable methods and tools.

The purpose of this book is to develop a better understanding of the problem of performance evaluation and to analyze available techniques within this concept. The book is directed to present and future computer analysts and designers. The readers are assumed to be familiar with concepts of hardware organization, system architecture, and operating systems. The readers are exposed to many different ideas and trends, but the level of detail is kept relatively low; for details, the readers are directed to appropriate publications.

This work is a result of a three-year experience in measuring and analyzing the performance of a developing system as well as teaching the subject at Stanford and Columbia Universities. It is based on my dissertation completed in June 1974 carrying the same name. However, after an additional year and a half of research and teaching, the original material was largely restructured and enriched with new ideas. While not intended to be a textbook, this book can nevertheless serve as a basic text for a self-contained course or seminar on computer performance evaluation, supplemented from the numerous references where more depth is desirable. At Stanford, the material was concentrated into a four-week course offered as a part of a special summer program to qualified people from outside companies. At Columbia University, the material was used in a one-semester graduate seminar with summary lectures supplemented by students' presentations of selected papers.

The book has two parts. The first part presents the fundamental concepts (Chapters 1 and 2); the second part examines different techniques and tools in detail (Chapters 3 to 6). Chapter 1 presents a brief overview of the need for performance evaluation, describes the levels of a computer system, and defines the boundary between the system and the system environment. Chapter 2 defines and examines the performance evaluation problem: specification of system workload, selection of performance measures, determination of the quantitative values of performance measures, and evaluation of performance. Chapter 3 is dedicated to system models. A functional model provides a framework for system analysis; a performance model describes the effect of the system structure and the system workload on system performance. A performance model can be obtained analytically, by simulation, or by direct measurement. Chapter 4 discusses workload models for measurement and simulation experiments. Chapter 5 looks at simulation techniques. Chapter 6 evaluates measurement techniques and tools. Chapter 7 deals with the problems of computer measurability and performance control. A case study of system instrumentation for measuring CPU utilization profile, multiprogramming effect, and utilization and efficiency of program modules is presented in the Appendix. Each chapter has its own bibliography that includes selected articles, reports, and books relevant to the covered subject.

I would like to express my deep gratitude to the editor of this series, Professor E.J. McCluskey of Stanford University, who suggested a publication of this material in book form. His encouragement and constructive comments were always greatly appreciated. Many valuable comments and suggestions came from Professor Forest Baskett of Stanford University. I am also indebted to my students who helped me to clarify many of the concepts presented here. I owe many thanks to Joanne Knowlton for her excellent typing job and cheerful support in the iterative process of polishing the manuscript. Finally, my warm thanks belong to my husband for his understanding and his supportive belief that one day this book will indeed come out.

Chapter 1

Introduction

In the history of science, there are two converging avenues
along which flows the potential of progress: the avenue of
ideas and the avenue of techniques. It is the confluence of
these that has made possible the marvels of modern
civilization.

P.P. Schodeberk
Management Systems

Computer performance evaluation is a complex process that involves many analyses and decisions. At the very root of the problem lies the question: What are the legitimate measures of performance? Once these measures are specified, it is then necessary to decide what techniques to use in order to determine their values, analyze what factors have the greatest effect on performance, and qualitatively assess performance given the values of performance measures.

The computer as a system can be analyzed and evaluated by standard techniques used to analyze and evaluate systems in other fields of science and engineering. Such techniques include simulation, queuing theory, statistical methods of sampling, estimation, regression analysis, experimental design and hypothesis testing, optimization techniques, control theory, decision making methods, etc. The true information about a system's behavior in a given environment can only be obtained by measurement. Without measurement, no performance hypothesis can be fully validated. Measurement is thus viewed as a fundamental technique.

This book is concerned mainly with the effectiveness of various techniques and tools available to a computer performance evaluator. Since, like other disciplines, the discipline of computer hardware and software engineering had to develop its own measurement techniques and tools, special attention will be given in this book to the design of measurement tools and system instrumentation.

1.1 NEED FOR PERFORMANCE EVALUATION

The development of computer performance evaluation as a separate discipline is a natural result following the development of powerful and complex computer systems.

The early computers were designed to be operated by the programmer himself, who in fact could actually watch what was going on in the computer during program execution. In the early days of computers software was practically nonexistent, and the fundamental design decisions were concerned with the word size together with the composition and implementation of the machine instruction set. Computer evaluation and comparison were based on such parameters as the CPU cycle time and the execution times of the basic instructions (usually the ADD instruction). Various software aids such as assemblers and compilers only became feasible with the subsequent development of larger and less expensive memories. Together with better peripherals, this led to the introduction of batch processing controlled by a resident supervisor. Software was discovered to have a great impact on the ease of programming. Mere instruction speeds and instruction repertoire could not sufficiently describe qualities of new computer systems. Software characteristics had to be taken into consideration too. Together the system overhead, the compile speed, and the execution speed determined how long a specific program would take to run. To make programming easier was not the only reason behind the efforts in software development. As more powerful (and more expensive) hardware became available, greater pressure was applied to increase the efficiency of computer operations and to achieve better utilization of various computer system units. Independent I/O channels communicating with the central processor via an interrupt system allowed concurrent usage of several machine resources (overlap of CPU operations with I/O operations). The amount of overlap was not easily detectable, yet it was an important parameter in determining system throughput. Multiprogramming further increased the chance of good system utilization, but it became increasingly difficult to understand and to follow what was happening inside the system. The question 'How long does it take to execute a given job' no longer had a simple answer. Job execution time under a heavy over-all system load could be several times that achieved when such a job was the only one in the system. More had to be learned about internal system operations, such as scheduling algorithms, resource allocation policies, etc. Time-sharing, interactive processing and real-time processing only enhanced the need for further analysis.

Early performance evaluation studies were concerned with comparing the capabilities of different computers. This still remains one of the major purposes of performance evaluation, but such a study now requires more sophisticated methods. Because of the large investments in installed computer equipment and the high cost of running a computer center, today considerable attention is paid to the possibilities of increasing system efficiency through hardware configuration changes and software changes. The high cost of software development and hardware design creates pressure for evaluating proposed systems and system changes before the actual implementation begins.

The frequently cited classification scheme by Lucas [LUCA71] divides performance evaluation undertakings into selection evaluation, performance monitoring, and performance projection. Lucas' classification scheme closely reflects the reasons given in the preceding paragraph. For a discussion of *methods* of performance evaluation, it is generally better to use a classification scheme that differentiates between comparative evaluation and analytic evaluation. These differing approaches are defined as follows.

1. **Comparative Evaluation** Performance of a particular computer system is evaluated relative to the performance of another computer system. The purpose of such an evaluation may be to:

(a) Lease or purchase new hardware and software,
(b) Select a supplier of computing services,
(c) Classify existing systems,
(d) Evaluate changes in system hardware or software (i.e., compare performance of the modified system with performance of the system prior to modification).

2. **Analytic Evaluation** Performance of a computer system is evaluated with respect to various system parameters and system workload. The purpose of such evaluation may be to:

(a) Improve performance of an existing system (performance tuning),

(b) Maintain performance of an operating system within specified limits (performance control),

(c) Design and implement new systems.

1.2 COMPUTER AS A MULTI-LEVEL SYSTEM

A system is a structure that is composed of elements connected according to some interconnection rules. An element of a system can itself in turn be a system that is composed of some lower-level elements. It is necessary to decide a level at which to analyze the system. The elements of a system are then those systems that are considered to be indivisible at the chosen level.

Computer hardware can be discussed on several levels [BELC71]: the circuit level, the register-transfer (RT) level, the programming level, and the processor memory switch (PMS) level. The elements of the RT level are circuits representing registers, shifters, adders, etc. The systems arising from this level are controllers, processors, and interfaces. The programming level, sometimes called the instruction set processor (ISP) level, adds to the RT system the capability of executing instructions from a stored program. Finally, the elements of the PMS level are complex hardware units such as processors, memories, controllers, and switches. These elements are linked together by switches that govern flows of information.

For a user who is interested in the computer as a problem-solving tool and data processing utility, bare hardware does not represent a complete system. The desired services are provided by the operating software (OS) level that is an extension to the hardware hierarchy. The quality of services is, of course, influenced by the hardware system. Hardware speed limits the speed with which users' requests can be processed and indirectly imposes boundaries on what services are feasible. The ISP and PMS levels provide an interface between the hardware that does the actual work and the software that maps different applications into executable tasks. The operating software is again a hierarchy of several levels [TSIC74]. The kernel of the operating software controls the PMS switches. Additional levels of the operating software add progressively more power and flexibility:

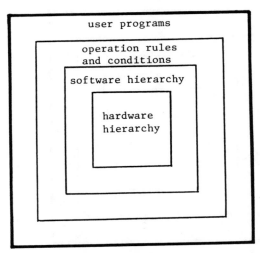

Figure 1.1.   Levels of the information processing system.

automatic scheduling and resource allocation, data base management, compiling, linking, and loading of programs, command structure. The highest level of consideration is the level at which the user communicates with the system. At this level, the system elements are the processes that carry out the functions requested by the user.

Performance of a system is determined by the performance of individual system elements and the way these elements are connected into a system. Thus, any and all of the described levels contribute toward the performance seen by the user. In order to meet specific performance objectives, all of these levels have to be taken into consideration in an evaluation of performance.

In addition to specifying the level at which the system is to be evaluated, it is necessary to make a clear distinction between the system and its environment, that is, to define the system boundary.[1] For example, the system may be defined merely as the hardware operating in the environment created by the software. Or the system of interest may be a specific hardware or software subsystem operating in the environment of other hardware and software subsystems

---

[1] The system boundary can change during the course of system evaluation. An instructive example can be found in [STIM74], where the boundary is called the evaluation interface.

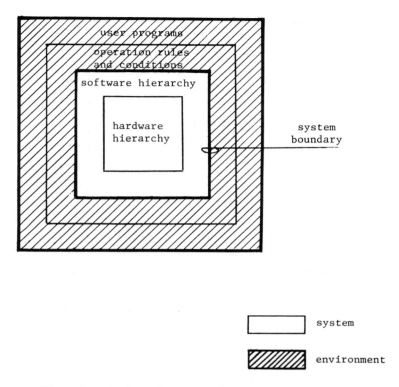

Figure 1.2.   Evaluated system and its environment.

with which it interacts. Or the system can be perceived as a total complex organization of hardware, software, user programs, users, programmers and operators, together with the operation rules and conditions governing the interactions of the human with the non-human elements (job submitting policies, handling of tapes and disk packs requested by a job, equipment layout, etc.). The system hierarchy has to be thus extended by additional levels as shown in figure 1.1. This complete system will be called the information processing system. The information processing system is in turn an element of a higher level organization such as a company, a university, or a bank. Unless otherwise specified, the performance of a computer system will be discussed with respect to the user interface as shown in figure 1.2.

BIBLIOGRAPHY

Entries marked with an asterisk (*) are referenced in the text.

BAUW72   Bauer, W.F., Rosenberg, A.M., "Software—Historical Perspectives and Current Trends", *AFIPS Proc. FJCC,* 1972, pp. 993–1007.

*BELC71   Bell, C.G., Newell, A., *Computer Structures: Readings and Examples,* McGraw-Hill Book Company, Inc., 1971, Chapter 1.

KNIG66   Knight, K.E., "Changes in Computer Performance: A Historical Review", *Datamation,* Vol. 12, No. 9, September 1966, pp. 40–54.

KNIG68   Knight, K.E., "Evolving Computer Performance 1963–1967," *Datamation,* Vol. 14, No. 1, January 1968, pp. 31–35.

*LUCA71   Lucas, H.C., "Performance Evaluation and Monitoring", *Computing Surveys,* Vol. 3, No. 3, September 1971, pp. 79–90.

*STIM74   Stimler, S., *Data Processing Systems: Their Performance, Evaluation, Measurement, and Improvement,* Stimler Associates, Moorestown, New Jersey, 1974.

*TSIC74   Tsichritris, D.C., Bernstein, P.A., *Operating Systems,* Academic Press, 1974.

WILK72   Wilkes, M.V., "Historical Perspectives—Computer Architecture", *AFIPS Proc. FJCC,* 1972, pp. 971–976.

Chapter 2

Computer System Performance

The very fundamental problem of computer performance analysis is the problem of defining "performance" and of defining criteria for performance evaluation. First, it must be understood that performance is a qualitative characteristic, highly subjective to the needs of the people involved with the system. Thus within the community of computer system designers, programmers, users, managers, and operators, computer system "performance" has many different interpretations. Loosely defined, "*performance* is the degree to which a computing system meets the expectations of the person involved with it" [DOHE70]. Such "expectations," however, may far exceed the capabilities of the system in question. The following definition excludes such cases: "*performance* . . . is the effectiveness with which the resources of the host computer system are utilized toward meeting the objectives of the software system" [GRAH73]. The former definition can be paraphrased as "How well does the system enable me to do what I want to do?", while the latter can be interpreted as "How well does the system do what it is intended to do?".

At this point, it is necessary to emphasize the difference between evaluating a system as opposed to evaluating performance of a system. Performance is only one point of view from which a system may be evaluated. The primary aspects of system evaluation are the functional features of the system such as the mode of operation (interactive, batch, virtual machine), types of peripheral devices supported by the system, the size of directly addressable memory, languages supported by the system, data base management facilities, and so forth. Given that the system has the features needed for a specific application, the next question is the system's performance for this application. Other related aspects are the ease of use of different system mechanisms and services, support from the manufacturer, the cost of the system. System evaluation then involves evaluation of various trade-offs such as features vs. cost, or performance vs. cost, or performance vs. ease of use. This book concentrates on the problems and process of actual performance evaluation.

Performance of a system can be discussed from two different positions: first, the effectiveness with which the system handles a specific application; and second, the internal efficiency of the system. Effectiveness is what is seen by the system user. Efficiency is how the system uses its resources in order to process the respective workload. System effectiveness is, of course, influenced by this internal efficiency. However, the effectiveness of system S_1 with respect to a certain application may be much better than that of system S_2, yet S_2 may be using its resources much more efficiently than S_1.

The system components influence system performance through their own characteristics and through their mutual interaction. Performance of individual components is usually measured by their speed. However, as the system components are put together, their maximum speed can rarely be fully utilized due to:

1. Insufficient speed or capacity of some of the system components that prevent other system components from operating at their maximum speeds.
2. Interference caused by simultaneous demands of two or more system components to communicate with a particular component where these demands can be processed only sequentially.
3. Characteristics of the system workload.

The system performance is a function of the performance of the individual components, as well as the above factors.

The process of performance evaluation must start with selecting a proper set of parameters upon which the evaluation will be based. These parameters are called performance measures. The evaluation process consists then of the following steps:

1. Define performance measures.
2. Determine the quantitative values of performance measures and analyze system performance with respect to system structure and system workload.
3. Assign qualitative values to different levels of performance measures and assess system performance.

2.1 SYSTEM WORKLOAD

Performance of a system can be discussed only in the context of what the system is required to do. Users' applications, once translated into programs and commands, can be characterized by the type and the amount of resources[1] the system will have to allocate to execute these programs and commands. The total of resource demands generated by the user community represents the system workload.

Examples of parameters used to describe computer system workload are presented in Table 2.1. The references given in this table are examples of the types of studies where such characterization is used.

In most computer installations, the instantaneous workload changes quite unpredictably. This is especially true for interactive systems. The speed of the user's response plays an important role in what load is generated at individual system entry points; this human factor only enhances the unpredictability of workload changes. It is this uncontrollable fluctuation of the system workload that makes the evaluation of system performance so difficult. Without understanding the workload, performance analysis and prediction is at best inaccurate, possibly completely invalid.

Generally, the workload of a computer system has certain statistical properties that do not change over reasonably long time periods. It is then possible to:

1. Characterize the workload by distributions of demands made on individual system resources.
2. Define a unit of work and express the workload as a number of such units.

Quantification of workload by work units is used when defining and comparing system processing capabilities. A unit of work is assumed to require a fixed but not necessarily explicitly known quantity of computation. Generally, it is very difficult to define a

---

[1] For the discussion of system performance, the resources of a system are the individual system components. System components are reusable resources. The second type of resources is consumable resources such as a message or an activation record of a called procedure [COFF73]. The latter type is not considered here.

unit of work. Even when programs are broken down to very elementary operations (e.g., instructions), the characteristics of such elementary operations differ.

The characterization of workload by demands made on system resources can also be used to define a unit of work. In fact, the workload parameters given in Table 2.1 are already defined with respect to a specific logical unit processed by a computer system. Such a logical unit is often adopted as a unit of work. To satisfy the requirement that a unit of work represents a fixed quantity of computation, this logical unit is afixed with characteristics representing the mean of characteristics of all such units processed by the system. Examples of units of work with references to how these units are used in performance evaluation are given in Table 2.2.

The most rigorous approach is to determine the exact amount of computation necessary to perform a certain task. The quantity of computation can be defined in terms of information entropy [ROZW73, JOHR72]. The entropy measure $H(X_i)$ of the system component X_i with n_i possible states is

$$H(X_i) = - \sum_{j=1}^{n_i} p_{ij} \log_2 p_{ij},$$

where p_{ij} is the probability of X_i being in state j. The amount of computational work a particular task represents to a system S is then a sum of entropies of all components X_i of system S that are involved in the computational process.

Workload characterization must be selected in accordance with the type of the evaluation project. Effectiveness of the system at the user's interface is evaluated in terms of what the system does for the user, not how much computational work is required or how system resources are used. This is especially important when comparing two or more different systems since the same job usually represents different resource demands when run on different systems. However, when studying the efficiency of the system, the demands made on individual system resources must be explicitly known. Finally, the entropy measure of computational work allows one to compare the effectiveness of different hardware organizations and programming practices.

Table 2.1
Workload Characterization

Workload Parameters	Description	Reference
Job CPU time	Total CPU time requested by a single job[a]	DEME69, MCDO70, SEKI73, SREE74, WATS71
Job I/O requests	Total number of I/O operations requested by a single job	MCDO70, SREE74, WATS71
CPU service time	CPU time required to process a single CPU task	ESTRA67A, FULL75A, KIMB72A, KLEI68, PRIC72, SVOB73A
I/O service time	I/O time required to process a single I/O task	FULL75A, MCDO70, PRIC72, SVOB73A
Interarrival time	Time between two successive requests for a system service	DEME69, ESTR67A, FULL75A, MCDO70, PRIC72
Priority	Priority assigned to a job by the user	ESTR67A
Blocked time	Time a job is incapable of receiving CPU service	KIMB72A
Memory requests	Amount of memory requested by a single job	DOHE70, MCDO70, SEKI73, SHEM72, WATS71

Working set size	Number of pages of a single job that must be kept in the main memory	COFF72, DEME69, DOHE70
Locality of reference	Time for which all memory references made by a single job remain within a single page or a set of pages	DOHE70, SEKI73
User response time	Time needed by a user at an interactive terminal to generate a new request (think and type time)	DEME69, ESTR67A, KLEI68, SVOB73A
User intensity	Processing time per request/ user response time	SHEM72
Number of simultaneous users	Number of interactive users logged concurrently	DEME69, SHEM72, SVOB73A
Number in the system	Number of jobs or tasks being serviced or waiting in queues for system resources	ESTR67A, SEKI73
Instruction mix	Relative frequencies of different types of instructions the system must execute	CORS70, SALI73

[a]In an interactive system, each command issued from a user's terminal is assumed to represent a new job.

Table 2.2
Examples of Units of Computer Work

Work Unit	Description	Reference
Job	A job[a] with demand characteristics (CPU time, I/O, memory) that are representative of demand characteristics of the jobs processed by a particular system	BROT74, ERIK74, SHEM72, STIM74
Task	An operation that is representative of operations carried out by a particular processor (CPU, I/O channel)	ESTR67A, TEOR72
Instruction	An instruction with demand characteristics (execution time, instruction length, memory references, local registers used) that are representative of demand characteristics of the instructions of a particular instruction set processor	LEAV74, RAIC64
Bit	Unit of information gain	ROZW73, JOHR72

[a]In an interactive system, each command issued from a user's terminal is assumed to represent a new job.

2.2 PERFORMANCE MEASURES

Performance is characterized by a set of quantitative parameters—performance measures. The effectiveness of a system is described in terms of the capability to process a given workload, and the capability to meet time requirements of individual users. The efficiency is measured by internal delays and utilization of individual system components vs demand. Effectiveness measures are the prime performance measures. Values of these measures can be assessed from observations made at the external side of the evaluation interface: they are what is seen by the system users. (These measures are frequently called external performance measures.) Efficiency is an internal factor. Values of efficiency measures usually must be obtained from within the system. These measures aid in identifying problems that diminish system effectiveness.

Examples of both external and internal performance measures are given in Table 2.3. Included are the most frequently used measures, as well as some interesting measures used in only one or a very few studies. The column USE indicates where a particular measure may be of interest in regard to the classification given in Chapter 1. The references are selected examples of studies that demonstrate different uses and different ways of obtaining the value of a particular measure.

Performance measures are most frequently expressed as mean values. In many cases, mean values are clearly inadequate measures of system performance. For example, if the variance of the response time of an interactive system is large, the user cannot develop a working rhythm. He is likely to be unsatisfied with the system performance even if the mean response time is reasonably short. Thus, if the exact distribution of the response time is not known, at least the variance of the response time ought to be considered as a performance measure in addition to the mean response time. A good measure of performance of an interactive system is the percentile response time. N percentile response time is defined as the time limit that guarantees that the response times of N percent of all requests are shorter than this limit [SEKI72]. One cannot expect the response time for very involved requests to be as short as the response time for trivial requests. Thus, response time (percentile response time) should be assessed separately for different classes of requests. In this aspect, the external delay factor (Table 2.3) is a more realistic measure.

In conclusion, performance measures can be specified only with respect to the type and the purpose of the evaluated system, its workload, and the purpose of evaluation. Performance measures must be well defined, since they set a framework for the entire evaluation process.

2.3 MEASUREMENT AND ANALYSIS

Having selected performance measures, the crucial problem is to determine how these performance measures depend on the system workload and the system structure. An understanding of such a

Table 2.3
Examples of Performance Measures

Performance Measure	Description	Use	Reference
	SYSTEM EFFECTIVENESS		
Throughput	Amount of useful work completed per unit of time with given workload	1a, 1c, 1d 2a, 2b, 2c	BARD71, DOHE70, KERN72, KIMB72A, PRIC72, SEKI73, SHEM72, STIM74
Relative throughput	Elapsed time required to process given workload on system S_1 / elapsed time required to process the same workload on system S_2	1a, 1c, 1d 2a	DRUM73, HANS71, STIM74
Capability (capacity)	Maximum amount of useful work that can be performed per unit of time with given workload	1a, 1c, 1d 2a, 2b, 2c	CORS70, KUCK76, STIM74
Turnaround time	Elapsed time between submitting a job[a] to a system and receiving the output	1a, 1b, 1d 2a, 2b, 2c	KIMB72A, STRA72, STIM74
Response time	Turnaround time of requests and transactions in an interactive or a real time system	1a, 1b, 1d 2a, 2b, 2c	DEME69, DOHE70, ESTR67A, GROC72, SEKI72
Availability	Percentage of time a system is available to users	1a, 1b, 1d 2a, 2c	DRUM73, GROC72, KIMB72A

SYSTEM EFFICIENCY

External delay factor	Job turnaround time/ job processing time	1a, 1b, 1d 2a, 2b, 2c KERN72
Elapsed time multiprogramming factor (ETMF)	Turnaround time of a job under multiprogramming/turnaround time of this job when it is the only job in the system	1d, 2a, 2c SHEM72, STIM74
Gain factor	Total system time[b] needed to execute a set of jobs under multiprogramming/total system time needed to execute the same set sequentially	1d, 2a, 2c KERN72
CPU productivity	Percent of time a CPU is doing useful work (used as a measure of throughput)	1d, 2a, 2b, 2c BARD71, HANS71, PRIC72, RODR72, SEKI73
Component overlap	Percent of time two or more system components operate simultaneously	1d, 2a, 2b, 2c DRUM73, HOFF73
System utility	Weighted sum of utilization of system resources	1d, 2a, 2b, 2c PEWI73

Continued

Table 2.3–*Continued*

Performance Measure	Description	Use	Reference
Overhead	Percent of CPU time required by the operating system	1d, 2a, 2c	BARD71, SEKI73
Internal delay factor	Processing time of a job under multiprogramming/processing time of this job when it is the only job in the system	1d, 2a, 2c	KERN72
Reaction time	Time between entering the last character on a terminal or receiving the input in the system and receiving first CPU quantum	1d, 2a, 2b, 2c	ANDE72, SHEM72
Wait time for I/O	Elapsed time required to process an I/O task	1d, 2a, 2c	FULL75A, SVOB73A
Wait time for CPU	Elapsed time required to process a CPU task	1d, 2a, 2c	ESTR67A, SVOB73A
Page fault frequency	Number of page faults per unit of time	1d, 2a, 2b, 2c	DOHE70, RODR72

[a]In an interactive system, each command issued from a user's terminal is assumed to represent a new job.
[b]System time is the time when at least one of the system's processors (CPU, channels) is busy.

relationship is essential if performance optimization efforts are to be constructive, but it is also important when selecting a new computer system. An expression of this relationship is the performance model of the system. The performance model is the ultimate goal of system analysis.

The values of performance measures are determined by a combination of the following:

1. Measurement
2. Analysis
3. Simulation

The most accurate values are obtained when the system is measured under its real workload. Because of the variability or unavailability of the real workload, it is often necessary to design an artificial reproducible workload and measure the system performance against this artificial workload. Whenever evaluating a system that has not yet been implemented or is otherwise unavailable for measurement, it is necessary to develop a functional model of that system. The values of performance measures are then obtained either by analytical means or by simulation.

Measurement and modeling are complementary processes:

1. A model provides a framework for measurement;
2. Measurement provides data for validating the model;
3. The model aids in testing hypothesis and finding solutions to performance problems;
4. Correctness of model predictions is finally verified by measurement.

This section is only a very brief outline of the area that accounts for most of the effort in computer performance evaluation. A set of tools has to be developed for system performance evaluation. These tools can be described in four categories: system models, workload models, simulators, and performance monitors. The concepts, utility, applicability, and implementation of different techniques and tools are to be elaborated in the following chapters.

2.4 CONTROL OF SYSTEM PERFORMANCE

Listing of all parameters that affect computer system performance would be an exceedingly difficult task. As a crude generalization, performance of a computer system with respect to a specific application is a function of:

- System configuration
- Resource management policies of the operating system
- Efficiency of system programs
- Effectiveness of the instruction set processor
- Speed of hardware components

Performance characteristics are shaped in three stages:

1. System design
2. System implementation
3. Matching the system to a given workload

Since each information processing system is bound to handle a different workload, the last stage represents most of the performance evaluation and optimization efforts. This stage is concerned mainly with system configuration and resource management, that is, allocation and scheduling of PMS components.

Performance of a particular computer system installation can be controlled in several different ways:

- Adjustment of system control parameters
- Change or modification of resource management policies
- Balancing the distribution of load among system components through system reconfiguration (changes in the assignment of peripheral devices to channels or the assignment of files to physical storage devices, changes in the distribution of software components in the system memory hierarchy, etc.)
- Replacement or modification of system components

In general, the performance characteristics of the RT and the ISP levels are fixed during the implementation stage. Changes in software, however, are possible after the initial implementation. Efficiency of a program is determined by:

- Efficiency of the used algorithm
- Programming style
- Implementation language

Improving software efficiency (reducing system overhead) may yield more rewarding results than changes in resource management policies [DARD70, ROEK69].

As long as the user interface does not change, the system does not change to the user: only the performance does. However, viewed internally, configuration changes and software changes result in a new system, a system that has to be designed, analyzed, implemented, tested, and documented. Control parameters can be changed as needed without having to test the system operationally. Table 2.4 lists some system parameters that can be used to control system performance together with references that show how these parameters affect system performance. Control parameters may have to be set before the system is started, or may be changed during system operation. In the latter case, changes may have to be induced by the operator, or, as the most advanced feature, control parameters can be changed automatically in response to changing user requirements. Automatic performance control is discussed in Chapter 7.

Finally, turnaround time or response time measures not only the system performance but also the quality of the program that constitutes the job. Performance improvement with respect to a specific application ought to be approached from both sides: reducing the amount of work required by the application [FERR75, HATF71, KNUT71, NEME71], and improving the efficiency of the system.

2.5 QUALITATIVE ASSESSMENT OF SYSTEM PERFORMANCE

The numeric values of performance measures have to be translated into qualitative values. Let p_i be the value of the ith performance measure and let p_i' be the value of this measure for some reference system. It is necessary to define some scale of "goodness" for p_i and the relative measure p_i/p_i'. For the absolute value p_i, we want to

Table 2.4
Examples of Control Parameters

Control Parameter	Description	Reference
Quantum size	Time quantum in which the CPU of a time-sharing system is allocated to jobs[a]	ESTR67A, POTI76 SHEM72
Internal priority	Priority based on the demands of a job and services already received	BERN71, LYNC74
Degree of multiprogramming	Number of jobs that are simultaneously in the main memory and thus eligible to use the CPU	RODR72
Memory partition size	Amount of main memory allocated to a single job	COFF72, DOHE70
Window size	Time interval for determining the working set of a job	HEND74
Maximum allowed paging rate	Maximum allowed paging rate in a demand paging system	BARD76
Page survival index	Number of CPU bursts received by a program before an unreferenced page is removed from main memory	BARD75, BARD76
Number of simultaneous users	Number of terminal users logged into the system	ESTR67A, SHEM72
Device-to-channel assignment	Assignment of I/O devices to available channels	SMIT73

[a]In an interactive system, each command issued from a user's terminal is assumed to represent a new job.

know how satisfactory it is and if it can be further improved. Note that p_i may be optimal for the given system, yet from the user's standpoint, it may be unsatisfactory. When using the relative measure, we are interested in whether p_i represents a significant improvement over p_i'. It is very important to assess carefully the value of a performance improvement with respect to the cost of achieving such an improvement. For example, it was established that 20% degradation in system response time may easily go unnoticed by the system users [SALT70]. Would 20% improvement in response time have sufficient qualitative value to justify the cost of such an improvement? Or does the response time have to drop first below a certain limit before the improvement is acknowledged? The latter may be true if even after the improvement, the system response time is much longer than is comfortable for the system user. Tuning an underloaded system to increase its capacity is another example of futile effort.

Sometimes, improvement of system performance with respect to a particular performance measure is possible only at the cost of worsening performance with respect to some other measures. The qualitative value of a specific level of a performance measure is the user's preference for this level. Performance tradeoffs can be resolved only if the relative preferences for different levels of different performance measures are known. Determination of the preferred combinations is the basic problem of the decision theory.

Formal methods of utility theory were applied by Grochow to assess preferences of a group of users for different levels of three performance measures: availability, response time to trivial ("edit") requests, and response time to complex ("compile") requests [GROC72]. The preferences have to be assessed for each possible combination of values. Thus, this method is feasible only with a very small number of parameters and very small number of levels.

Erikson assessed system performance in terms of the cost of using the system [ERIK74]. The cost of using the system is a function of the system cost and the cost of the programmer. The higher the throughput, the lower is the system cost per unit of work. The shorter the response time, the less the programmer's time is wasted waiting for response and the lower is the cost of programming. As the system approaches its capacity (maximum throughput), the response time suffers. A proper balance between throughput and response time has to be established such that the cost of using the system is minimized.

An important factor that influences the productivity of a system user is the ease of using the system for a specific application. This factor has finally received more attention under the label "human engineering." The response time belongs to the category of human-oriented considerations; however, it is neither the only important consideration, nor the most important consideration. Ease of use and performance are frequently conflicting design requirements. Since both of these factors can make a user's task either satisfying or frustrating, there is no simple rule as to how to resolve the conflict.

BIBLIOGRAPHY

Entries marked with an asterisk (*) are referenced in the text.

*ANDE72   Anderson, H.A., Sargeant, R.G., "A Statistical Evaluation of the Scheduler of an Experimental Interactive Computing System", *Statistical Computer Performance Evaluation* (Editor: Freiberger, W.), Academic Press, 1972, pp. 73–98.

*BARD71   Bard, Y., "Performance Criteria and Measurement for a Time-Sharing System", *IBM Systems Journal,* Vol. 10, No. 3, 1971, pp. 193–214.

*BARD75   Bard, Y., "Application of the Page Survival Index (PSI) to Virtual Memory System Performance," *IBM Journal of Research and Development,* Vol. 19, No. 3, May 1975, pp. 212–220.

*BARD76   Bard, Y., "An Experimental Approach to System Tuning", *Proc. International Symposium on Computer Performance Modeling, Measurement and Evaluation,* March 1976, pp. 296–305.

BELT72A   Bell, T.E., Boehm, B.W., Watson, R.A., "Framework and Initial Phases for Computer Performance Improvement", *AFIPS Proc. FJCC,* 1972, pp. 1141–1154.

BELT73   Bell, T.E., "Performance Determination—The Selection of Tools, If Any", *AFIPS Proc. NCC,* 1973, pp. 31–38.

*BERN71   Bernstein, A.J., Sharp, J.C., "A Policy-Driven Scheduler for a Time Sharing System", *Communications of the ACM,* Vol. 14, No. 2, February 1971, pp. 74–78.

*BROT74   Brotherton, D.E., "The Computer Capacity Curve—A Prerequisite for Computer Evaluation and Improvement", *Proc. Second Annual SIGMETRICS Symposium on Measurement and Evaluation,* September 1974, pp. 166–179.

BUNY74   Bunyan, C.J. (Editor), Computer System Measurement, *Infotech State of the Art Report 18, 1974.*

CALI67   Calingaert, P., "System Performance Evaluation: Survey and Appraisal", *Communications of the ACM,* Vol. 10, No. 1, January 1967, p. 12–18.

*COFF72   Coffman, E.G., Ryan, T.A., "A Study of Storage Partitioning Using a Mathematical Model of Locality", *Communications of the ACM,* Vol. 15, No. 3, March 1972, pp. 185–190.

*COFF73   Coffman, E.G., Jr., Denning, P.J., *Operating Systems Theory,* Prentice-Hall, 1973.

*CORS70   Corsiglia, J., "Matching Computers to the Job—First Step Toward Selection", *Data Processing Magazine,* December 1970, pp. 23–27.

*DARD70   Darden, S.C., Heller, S.B., "Streamline Your Software Development", *Computer Decisions,* Vol. 2, No. 10, October 1970, pp. 29–33.

*DEME69   DeMeis, W.M., Weizer, N., "Measurement and Analysis of a Demand Paging Time-Sharing System", *Proc. 24th ACM National Conference,* 1969, pp. 201–216.

DENN73   Denning, P.J., "Why Our Approach to Performance Evaluation is SDRAWKCAB", *SIGMETRICS Performance Evaluation Review,* Vol. 2, No. 3, September 1973, pp. 13–16.

*DOHE70   Doherty, W.J., "Scheduling TSS/360 for Responsiveness," *AFIPS Proc. FJCC,* 1970, pp. 97–111.

*DRUM69   Drummond, M.E., "A Perspective on System Performance Evaluation," *IBM Systems Journal,* Vol. 8, No. 4, 1969, pp. 252–263.

*DRUM73   Drummond, M.E., *Evaluation and Measurement Techniques for Digital Computer Systems,* Prentice-Hall, 1973.

*ERIK74   Erikson, W.J., "The Value of CPU Utilization as a Criterion for Computer System Usage", *Proc. Second SIGMETRICS Symposium on Measurement and Evaluation,* September 1974, pp. 180–187.

*ESTR67A Estrin, G., Kleinrock, L., "Measures, Models and Measurements for Time-Shared Computer Utilities", *Proc. 22nd ACM National Conference,* 1967, pp. 85–96.

ESTR72   Estrin, G., Muntz, R.R., Uzgalis, R.C., "Modeling, Measurement and Computer Power", *AFIPS Proc. SJCC,* 1972, pp. 725–738.

*FERR75   Ferrari, D., "Tailoring Programs to Models of Program Behavior", *IBM Journal of Research and Development,* Vol. 19, No. 3, May 1975, pp. 244–251.

*FULL75A Fuller, S.H., Baskett, F., "An Analysis of Drum Storage Units", *Journal of the ACM,* Vol. 22, No. 1, January 1975, pp. 83–105.

*GRAM73   Graham, R.M., "Performance Prediction", *Advanced Course on Software Engineering,* Springer-Verlag, 1973, pp. 395–463.

*GROC72   Grochow, J.M., "Utility Functions for Time-Sharing System Performance Evaluation", *Computer,* September/October 1972, pp. 16–19.

GOOD72   Goodman, A.F., "Measurement of Computer Systems—An Introduction", *AFIPS Proc. FJCC,* 1972, pp. 669–680.

*HANS71   Hansemann, F., Kistler, W., Schulz, H., "Modeling for Computer Center Planning", *IBM Systems Journal,* Vol. 10, No. 4, 1971, pp. 305–324.

*HATF71   Hatfield, D.J., Gerald, J., "Program Restructuring for Virtual Memory", IBM Systems Journal, Vol. 10, No. 3, 1971, pp. 168–192.

HELL75   Hellerman, H., Conroy, T.E., *Computer System Performance,* McGraw-Hill Book Company, Inc., 1975.

*HEND74   Henderson, G., Rodriguez-Rosell, J., "The Optimal Choice of Window Sizes for Working Set Dispatching", *Proc. Second SIG-METRICS Symposium on Measurement and Evaluation,* September 1974, pp. 10–33.

*HOFF73   Hoffman, J.M., "Device Gain—A Measure of System Component Simultaneous Operation", *Proc. ACM Annual Conference,* 1973, pp. 320–326.

JOHR70   Johnson, R.R., "Needed: A Measure for Measure", *Datamation,* Vol. 16, No. 17, December 15, 1970, pp. 22–30.

*JOHR72   Johnson, R.R., "Some Steps Toward an Information System Performance Theory", *ACM SICME Performance Evaluation Review,* No. 3, 1972, pp. 4–15.

KARU71   Karush, A.D., "Performance Measurement", *Data Management,* July 1971, pp. 36–40.

*KERN72   Kerner, H., Kuemmerle, K., "Performance Measures, Definitions and Metric", *Proc. Sixth Annual Princeton Conference on Information Sciences and Systems,* March 1972, pp. 213–217.

*KIMB72A   Kimbleton, S.R., "Performance Evaluation—A Structured Approach", *AFIPS Proc. SJCC,* 1972, pp. 411–416.

*KLEI68   Kleinrock, L., "Certain Analytic Results for Time-Shared Processors", *Proc. IFIPS 1968,* pp. 838–845.

*KNUT71   Knuth, D.E., "An Empirical Study of FORTRAN Programs", Software—Practice and Experience, Vol. 1, No. 1, 1971, pp. 105–133.

*KUCK76   Kuck, D.J., Kumar, B., "A System Model for Computer Performance Evaluation," *Proc. International Symposium on Computer Performance Modeling, Measurement and Evaluation,* March 1976, pp. 187–199.

*LEAV74   Leavitt, D., "UK Tests Show Some Minis Outperform Bigger CPUs", *Computerworld,* Vol. 8, No. 52, December 1974, pp. 1–2.

*MCDO70   MacDougall, M.H., "Computer System Simulation: An Introduction", *Computing Surveys,* Vol. 2, No. 3, September 1970, pp. 191–209.

*NEME71   Nemeth, A.G., Rovner, P.D., "User Program Measurement in a Time-Shared Environment", *Communications of the ACM,* Vol. 14, No. 10, October 1971, pp. 661–666.

*PEWI73   Pewitt, T.C., Su, S.Y.W., "Resource Demanded Paging and Dispatching to Optimize Resource Utilization in an Operating System", *Proc. First Annual SICME Symposium on Measurement and Evaluation,* February 1973, pp. 29–36.

*POTI76   Potier, D., Gelenbe, E., Lenfant, J., "Adaptive Allocation of Central Processing Unit Quanta", *Journal of the ACM,* Vol. 23, No. 1, January 1976, pp. 97–102.

*PRIC72   Price, T.G., "An Analysis of Central Processor Scheduling in Multiprogrammed Computer Systems", *Technical Report No. 57,* Digital Systems Laboratory, Stanford University, Stanford, California, October 1972.

*RAIC64   Raichelson, E., Collins, G., "A Method for Comparing the Internal Operating Speeds of Computer", *Communications of the ACM,* Vol. 7, No. 5, May 1964, pp. 309–311.

*RODR72   Rodriquez-Rosell, J., Dupuy, J., "The Evaluation of a Time-Sharing Page Demand System", *AFIPS Proc. SJCC,* 1972, pp. 759–765.

*ROEK69   Roek, D.J., Emerson, W.C., "A Hardware Instrumentation Approach to Evaluation of a Large Scale System", *Proc. 24th ACM National Conference,* 1969, pp. 351–367.

*ROZW73   Rozwadowski, R.T., "A Measure for the Quantity of Computation", *Proc. First SICME Symposium on Measurement and Evaluation,* February 1973, pp. 100–111.

*SALI73   Salisbury, A.B., "The Evaluation of Microprogrammable Computer Architectures", *Technical Report No. 59,* Digital Systems Laboratory, Stanford University, Stanford, California, July 1973.

*SALT70   Saltzer, J.H., Gintell, J.W., "The Instrumentation of Multics", *Communications of the ACM,* Vol. 13, No. 8, August 1970, pp. 495–500.

*SEKI72   Sekino, A., "Performance Evaluation of Multiprogrammed Time-Shared Computer Systems", *Technical Report MAC TR-103,* MIT, Cambridge, Massachusetts, September 1972.

*SEKI73   Sekino, A., "Throughput Analysis of Multiprogrammed Virtual-Memory Computer Systems", *Proc. First Annual SICME Sym-*

posium on Measurement and Evaluation, February 1973, pp. 47–53.

*SHEM72   Shemer, J.E., Robertson, J.B., "Instrumentation of Time-Shared Systems", *Computer,* Vol. 5, No. 4, July/August 1972, pp. 39–48.

*SMIT73   Smith, A.J., "A Performance Analysis of Multiple Channel Controllers", *Proc. First Annual SICME Symposium on Measurement and Evaluation,* February 1973, pp. 37–46.

*SREE74   Sreenivasan, K., Kleinman, A.J., "On the Construction of a Representable Synthetic Workload", *Communications of the ACM,* Vol. 17, No. 3, March 1974, pp. 127–133.

*STIM74   Stimler, S., *Data Processing Systems: Their Performance, Evaluation, Measurement, and Improvement,* Stimler Associates, 1974.

*STRA72   Strauss, J.C., "A Benchmark Study", *AFIPS Proc. FJCC,* 1972, pp. 1225–1233.

*SVOB73A   Svobodova, L., "Online System Performance Measurements with Software and Hybrid Monitors", *Proc. ACM Fourth SICOPS Symposium on Operating System Principles,* October 1973, pp. 45–53.

*TEOR72   Teorey, T.J., "Properties of Disk Scheduling Policies in Multiprogrammed Computer Systems", *AFIPS Proc. FJCC,* 1972, pp. 1–11.

*WATS71   Watson, R., "Computer Performance Analysis: Applications of Accounting Data", *Report R-573-NASA/PR,* Rand Corporation, Santa Monica, California, May 1971.

Chapter 3

System Models

Computer system performance, as mentioned in the previous chapters, can be studied on many different levels. At each level, different parameters, different events and different relations characterize the system behavior and influence the system performance. Any analysis of a system is only an analysis of a certain model of the system. "A model is an abstraction containing only the significant variables and relations" [GRAH73A]. A model enables the analyst to concentrate on the important facts. Through a model, system operations stripped of the unnecessary detail are easier to understand. Such an understanding is essential for system analysis, system simulation, or system measurement.

In general, several different models are used during various stages of a performance evaluation project. These models can be divided into three general classes:

1. Structural models
2. Functional models
3. Performance models

A *structural model* describes individual system components and their connections. Such a model provides a useful interface between the real system and a more abstract model. A *functional model* describes how the system operates. A functional model defines the system such that the system can be analyzed mathematically or studied empirically. A *performance model* formulates the dependence of performance on the system workload and the system structure. A performance model is derived by analysis of a functional model for a specific model of workload.

Any system to be analyzed properly must be defined and understood to a sufficient level of detail. The level of detail in a model is an important factor. With too few details available, system performance cannot be properly assessed; too many details may conceal essential functions and relations. Adjustability of the level of detail in a system model to the needs of a project is an important consideration when selecting a representation medium.

The system and its interaction with its environment can be represented by a state model $y(t) = S[t_0,t,x,w]$, where w is the system input, y is the system output, and x is the system state at time $t \geqslant t_0$. This state model is the general form of the functional model used in performance analysis. As indicated earlier, the actual meaning of user's applications is irrelevant to performance analysis. System input is defined as the requests for system services; the output is the completed requests. The system state is the information the system needs to remember in order to be able to process all the input successfully. The system remains in the same state for a finite, in general non-zero, time interval. For performance analysis, it is necessary to observe only these discrete changes in the system state.

Analyses of computer system performance are usually concerned with the system operating in a "steady" state. A steady state is possible only in a statistical sense, that is, while the state x of the functional model changes according to immediate resource demands, the probability of being in any particular state does not change in time. The steady state performance model has the form $p = S_p(w)$, where p, the system performance, and w, the system workload, are characterized by stationary probability distributions and S_p represents the inner structure of the system.

One of the most serious problems in system modeling is proving the validity of a model, that is, proving that the model is an accurate representation of the evaluated system. A performance model is representative of the system in question if the two yield the same performance given the same workload. Validity of a model of a concrete existing system can be tested by comparing the performance predicted by the model with measured performance of the real system. But measurements are performed within a certain concept, that is, what is measured is again a model of the system, but more accurate and more detailed. By careful measurement, it may be possible to make the real system look like the model, but the value of such a model is more negative than positive. The system must be measured with all the deflections that occur under normal operating conditions and normal workload and the model must be made to fit this real system. Once a parallelism is achieved between the real system and its model, the model can be used as a predictive tool.

The most advanced function of a model is to prove feasibility of a system design and attainability of design objectives. System performance is studied on the model and the design is modified to meet the objectives [LASS72, GRAH73B]. Thus, a parallelism between the system and its model is the goal rather than a starting condition.

3.1 STRUCTURAL MODELS

A structural model is a description of the actual system components and their connections. Structural models are most frequently represented by block diagrams. The level of detail in a block diagram can easily be varied, since individual blocks can in turn be further laid down as self-contained block diagrams. Block diagrams generally show the paths of data flow as well as control flow, but they do not specify the conditions governing this flow. Thus, block diagrams are suitable only as the first general level description of the system under study.

Instead of using a graphical representation, a system can be described in a special language. The PMS notation was developed to provide a uniform description of system components and connections on the PMS level [SIEW74]; it is analogous to a block diagram. Based on this notation is PMSL, an interactive language that facilitates certain limited analysis of system reliability and performance [KNUD73]. Some computer system simulators, as discussed in Chapter 5, provide modeling languages that also belong to this category.

3.2 FUNCTIONAL MODELS

Functional models used in performance analysis can be divided into four groups:

1. Flowchart models
2. Finite-state models
3. Parallel nets
4. Queuing models

Flowchart models are suitable for studying program efficiency and execution time requirements. A flowchart model is a directed graph model where the nodes represent computational tasks and the arcs show the possible flow of control between tasks. Alternatively, the computational tasks may be viewed as being represented by the arcs, the nodes then being the branch and junction points in the modeled program, or merely points separating different tasks. Given the execution time of the individual tasks and the probability of following the various individual arcs, the total execution time of the modeled program can be derived by a sequence of elementary transformations [GRAH73A]. Performance figures can also be derived by simulating the flow through the model. Flowchart models of system components and users' programs can be used as building elements of a system model, tied together by a mechanism that simulates system resource allocation and scheduling [ANDJ76].

A finite-state model can be used for analysis of utilization of computer system resources [COOP71]. A finite-state model can be again represented by a directed graph; however, the nodes now represent the state of the system, the arcs represent the transitions between states. The system state is composed of the states of individual system components and it thus reflects concurrency of system operations. A simple finite-state model of resource utilization in a simple system with one CPU and one I/O channel is illustrated in figure 3.1. The fraction of time spent in individual system states is derived from the transitional probabilities assigned to individual arcs.

Parallel nets are modifications of Petri nets. Parallel nets are directed graphs made of two different types of nodes: transitions and places. Places with arcs directed into a transition are the conditions that must be satisfied concurrently if this transition is to occur. Under these conditions several transitions may occur simultaneously. Thus, Petri nets are well suited for describing concurrent asynchronous operations that take place in a computer system. In the original Petri nets, a transition is an event without duration [HOLT70]. In a real system, however, a transition is an operation with finite time duration. Timed Petri nets are a tool for analysis of system throughput [RAMA73]. Nutt describes modifications that further increase the practicality of Petri nets [NUTT72]. Such nets were found to be a useful aid in the design and implementation of a simulation model and in a planning of measurement experiments. An example of a timed Petri net is given in figure 3.2; conditions (places) are specified by circles, transitions by bars.

In a queuing models concept, a computer system is a set of

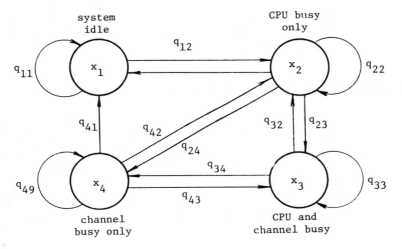

Figure 3.1. Finite-state model for analysis of CPU and channel utilization. q_{ij} = probability of a transition from state i to state j.

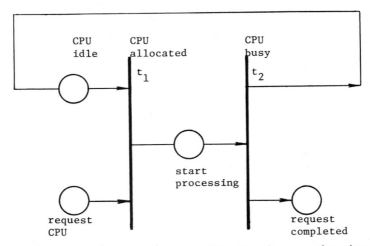

Figure 3.2. Timed Petri net representing CPU allocation. t_i = time duration of transition i.

resources and queues for these resources. When a job enters the system, it is placed in one of the queues where it waits until the requested resource becomes available. After a request has been processed, a job either leaves the system or enters some (possibly the same) queue again. Queuing models emphasize the flow of jobs through the system, but they also enable one to observe the state of the system. Queuing models are the most widely used models in computer performance analysis.

3.3 ANALYTICAL PERFORMANCE MODELS

An analytical performance model is a mathematical expression of the relation $p = S_p(w)$ that is derived by analysis of the behavior of a system's functional model. The underlying functional model must capture the basic structure of the system and the workload for which this model is analyzed must have the basic characteristics of the real workload, yet the model must be mathematically tractable. Representativeness and mathematical tractability of a model are conflicting requirements. The class of problems that is solvable with existing mathematical methods is very limited; many simplifying assumptions must be made even for the least complicated systems. Despite the forced simplifications, analytical models play an important role in performance analysis: they provide insight and a quick first-order approximation of system performance.

Analytical models often focus on the problem of management of a specific system resource: CPU scheduling [BASK71, ESTR67A, KLEI70A, MCKI69, PRIC72], scheduling of rotational I/O devices [FULL75A, TEOR72], management of hierarchical memories [CHAM73, COFF72, GHAN75, KIMB72B], channel scheduling [FULL73A, SMIT73, WILH73], buffer storage allocation [GAVE71], file organization [CHEN75, COLL70, DIET73]. Resource management policies are usually analyzed on a queuing model.[1] Whole time-sharing, multiprogramming, and multiprocessing systems can be approximated by queuing models of varying complexity:

---

[1] An excellent treatment of both basic and advanced methods and results of queuing theory applicable to computer performance analysis can be found in [KLEI75].

a single server model, a one-level queuing network, or a hierarchical queuing network.

The simplest model consists of a single processor (server) and a single queue of tasks to be processed by the processor (figure 3.3). Each task is described by two parameters: its time of arrival to the system and the requested service time. The workload of this simple system is specified by the distribution of the time between successive arrivals (interarrival time) and the distribution of the task service times. The system state is the number of tasks in the system. The performance measure for this system is the time a task spends in the system (the queuing time plus the service time). The following assumptions are made:

1. The interarrival times and service times are statistically independent
2. The successive interarrival times are statistically independent
3. All interarrival times are identically distributed
4. The service times for successive requests are statistically independent
5. All service times are identically distributed

Statistical independence does not in general hold within a single job [FULL71]. But if a multitude of jobs compete simultaneously for system resources, the successive requests are likely to belong to different jobs and are thus independent [ANDE72].

Additional assumptions must be made about the actual form of the interarrival time distribution and the service time distribution. In the simplest case, both distributions are assumed to be exponential. Exponential distributions are particularly desirable because of their "memoryless" or Markov property. The memoryless property means that at any time instant the probability that it will take n time units

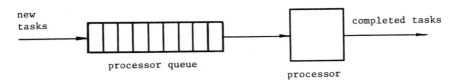

Figure 3.3. Simplest single-server model.

to complete the task in process is independent of the processing time the task has already received, or, that the probability of a new arrival is independent of the time of the last arrival. The assumption of exponential distributions greatly simplifies system analysis. The transient behavior of a system can be described by a set of ordinary differential equations and the steady state properties are represented by a set of linear homogeneous equations. The arrival process with the interarrival times exponentially distributed (Poisson process) was found to be a sufficiently good approximation of the real request pattern [ANDE72]. However, an exponential distribution of service times is a very poor approximation of the real world; more general distributions must be used to capture reality [FULL71, ANDE72]. Queuing systems with general distributions are much more difficult to analyze. The method of stages provides a useful approxim ition of a general distribution [BASK71]. An arbitrary distribution can be approximated arbitrarily closely by a set of stages such that the service times at each stage are exponentially distributed. Then the steady state characteristics of the system can be again described by a set of linear homogeneous equations.

Queuing models are further classified according to the service discipline, which is a rule that determines how the requests are processed. The simplest discipline is the first-come-first-served (FCFS) discipline where the requests are processed simply in the order of their arrival. More elaborate service disciplines were developed to increase system throughput and lower the total time a task spends in the system (turnaround time or response time). The round-robin (RR) discipline allocates one time quantum to a task at the head of the queue. If a task requires additional time after receiving its quantum, it is placed at the end of the queue. The model of a round-robin system is shown in figure 3.4. The limiting case of the round-robin discipline is the processor-sharing (PS) discipline where the service quantum approaches zero. If there are N tasks in the PS system, these N tasks receive equal service at the rate $1/N$ times the speed of the processor. In other scheduling disciplines, tasks are assigned priorities according to their service times. These priorities may change as a function of the time already received or a function of the time still required. Task's priority can also change as a function of task's waiting time [KLEI70A]. A comprehensive treatment of processor scheduling models can be found in [COFF73,

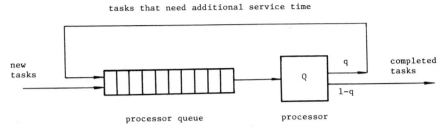

Figure 3.4. Round-robin model. Q = quantum size; q = probability that the task departing from the processor is not completed.

MCKI69, ESTR67A]. Some of the studied scheduling algorithms cannot be realized, either because of the physical limitations (processor-sharing discipline) or because the service times of tasks in a real system are not known in advance. However, these models provide an important insight of the impact and limits of processor scheduling in system performance.

Many of the processor scheduling models assume that the source of tasks is infinite. As long as the task arrival rate is lower than the rate at which tasks can be executed by the processor (service rate) the system does have a steady state where the expected number of tasks in the system is finite. If the arrival rate exceeds service rate, the queue grows infinitely long. In a time-sharing system, the maximum number of tasks competing for the CPU is the same as the maximum number of terminals that the system can support simultaneously. In a multiprogramming system, the maximum number of jobs eligible to use the CPU is limited to the number that can simultaneously reside in the main memory. A time-sharing system with a very large number of terminals can possibly be approximated by an infinite source model [BUZE74]. Multiprogramming systems and time-sharing systems with a small number of terminals must be represented by a finite source model. A finite source model is shown in figure 3.5. The workload of this model is composed of a fixed number of independent processes, each process consisting of an infinite number of cycles. In a time-sharing system, the cycle consists of processing the user's request and the user's think-type period. The peripheral processors are the users' terminals. In a multiprogramming system, the cycle consists of a CPU task and an I/O task. The peripheral processors are the I/O processors. In this simple model it is

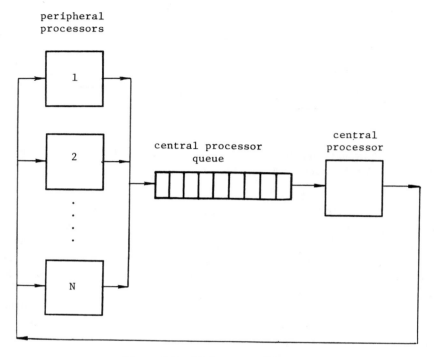

Figure 3.5. Finite-source model.

assumed that each active job is assigned an I/O processor, that is, the I/O processors are not shared. This assumption makes this model a rather poor representation of present multiprogramming computer systems where online secondary storage devices are shared by many users and where I/O processors frequently represent a major bottleneck.

Queuing may occur for any system resource that can be used by several active jobs, but only by one job at a time (CPU, channels, I/O controllers, disks and drums, memory blocks). Queuing may occur also at the interface between the system and its users (the system limits the number of simultaneous users). A complete system can be modeled as a network of interfacing queues. Most of the queuing networks are variations of the central server model that handles queuing for several different I/O processors [BUZE71]. This closed network, as shown in figure 3.6, is an extension of the finite source model. For some analyses, it is more appropriate to use an open

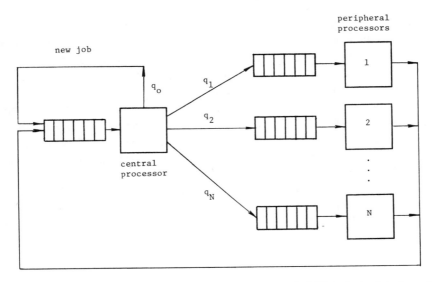

Figure 3.6. Central-server queuing network. q_o = probability that a job departing from the central processor is completed; q_i = probability that a job departing from the central processor requests peripheral processor i, where $i = 1, 2, \ldots, N$.

network model where new jobs can enter the system from an external source, provided that the system can accept an additional job. A general model for open, closed and mixed networks of queues was developed by Baskett *et al.* [BASK75]. The state of a queuing network is characterized by the number of tasks waiting at each server. The solution of a queuing network is the equilibrium joint probability distribution of these numbers. If all service times and interarrival times are exponentially distributed, each server and its queue can be analyzed independently. This technique of independent balance can be extended to networks with general service time distribution by using again the method of stages [BASK75]. The actual numerical solution of general queuing networks is aided by sophisticated algorithmic methods [HERZ75, REIS75, REIS76]. Approximate solution can be obtained by a method based on an analogue of Norton's theorem from circuits theory [CHAN75A, CHAN75B, SAVE75]. The method of diffusion approximation can be used for analysis of both the equilibrium and the transient behavior of queuing networks [KOBA74A, KOBA74B].

None of the models discussed so far dealt directly with the main memory. Queuing occurs also for the main memory, or better, for a place in the set of jobs eligible to use the memory. This factor is very difficult to incorporate into a queuing model, since a job uses the main memory simultaneously with other resources. Sekino developed a hierarchical model of a multiprogrammed, time-shared paging system where the queuing for the main memory occurs on the different level than CPU and I/O processing [SEKI72, SEKI73]. This model, shown in figure 3.7, was validated on the Multics system at MIT.

In a multiprocessor (multiple CPU) configuration, the use of the main memory must be studied on yet another level, across the hardware interface between the memory and the processors. This additional level is hidden under the "central processor" of figure 3.7. At this level, each memory module represents a separate server (figure 3.8). A queue for a memory module may build up if two or more processors make accesses to the same memory module. Analyti-

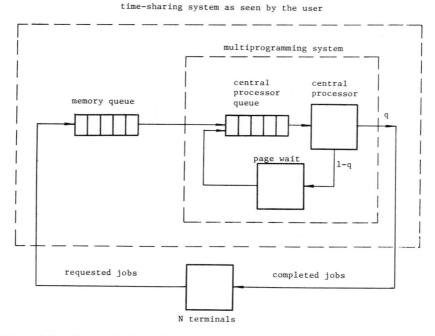

Figure 3.7. Hierarchical model of a multiprogrammed time-shared paging system. q = probability that a job departing from the central processor is completed.

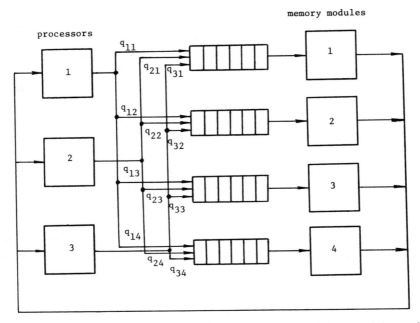

Figure 3.8. Queuing model of a multiprocessor system with a modular main memory. q_{ij} = probability that the memory access requested by processor i is to memory module j.

cal models have been developed to study memory conflicts in a multiprocessor system as a function of the system configuration and memory allocation strategies [BHAN75, SAST75].

An analytical model is a model of a class of systems. It can be used to study performance of any concrete system of the same class, by substituting proper numerical values for the model parameters. Once the model is validated on the real system, the numerical values of performance measures can be obtained with relatively little cost. This makes analytical models attractive as an aid in performance tuning [CHIU75, HUGP73, SEKI72, SHEM69] and planning of system growth [GIAM76, HANS71], but also as a decision element for automatic performance control in computer systems and networks.

3.4 EMPIRICAL PERFORMANCE MODELS

An empirical performance model is obtained by analysis of empirical data. As opposed to an analytical performance model, which is derived from a mathematical description of a specific functional model, an empirical model is constructed from observed values of performance measures p and observed workload characteristics w. The function S_p can be expressed in many different forms. The most frequently used representation is a table or a graph. The most desirable form is a closed-form mathematical expression.

3.4.1 Regression Models

Tsao and Margolin suggest that an empirical model should not be built on any preconceived theory, that is, significant variables and their relationship should emerge entirely from the observations [TSAO72]. A closed-form expression with these characteristics is derived by regression analysis.

The performance model is usually assumed to be linear. A general form of such model is

$$p_i = a_0 + \sum_{j=1}^{n} a_{ij}z_j ,$$

where the dependent variables p_i are the prime performance measures, the independent variables z_j are workload characteristics, system characteristics, or internal performance measures.[2] The assumption of linearity may contradict the results of analytical studies, but for a particular system and a particular purpose, it may be an acceptable approximation of an otherwise very complex relationship [SALT74].

Empirical regression models have been used mainly for postevaluation of hardware and software changes [BARD71, WALD73, WATS71]. The effects of a system modification on system performance have to be distinguished from the effects of possible changes in the system workload. Unless the workload effects are explicitly known, the evaluation of system changes must be performed in a controlled environment such that the system is always measured for the same workload. A good performance model eliminates the necessity of such controlled experiments.

---

[2] A detailed treatment of regression analysis techniques for estimating the model coefficients and evaluating the goodness of fit can be found in [DRAP68].

The process of evaluating computer system changes with a regression model consists of three steps:

1. Workload characteristics and system performance are measured before and after each modification.
2. Regression analysis techniques are used to construct a performance model or models.
3. The model is used to estimate to what extent the changes in performance are due to a system modification, and to what extent they are due to workload changes.

The effects of system changes can be observed in two different ways:

1. Introduce a modification variable z_m into the performance model:

$$p_i = a_0 + \sum_{j=1}^{n} a_{ij}z_j + a_{im}z_m .$$

The modification variable may describe the actual quantitative changes in some specific system parameters [WALD73], or simply a change ($z_m = 0$ before the modification, $z_m = 1$ after the modification [WATS72]). The changes in performance measures are determined directly from coefficients of the modification variable.
2. Construct separate models for the system before the modification and after the modification. The effect of the system modification is observed as changes in individual model coefficients [BARD71, TSAO72].

A regression model is calibrated to match one particular set of observations. A calibrated model must be validated, that is, it must be shown that this model represents the system behavior at all times. Validation is performed by testing the model with different sets of data. Validation of an empirical model is extremely important. It is possible to construct a linear model that fits one particular set of data even though the system is strongly non-linear. A different set of data, however, will result in a different model. While the system is non-linear with respect to its composed workload, it may be possible to achieve an acceptable linear approximation for separate classes of jobs [ANDE72]. Groups of observations that are subject to local linearization can be determined by cluster analysis.

The main drawback of the described method is the limited applicability of individual models. A model constructed purely by fitting empirical data may be a valuable tool for tuning the particular system, but the results can rarely be extended to other systems. A combination of an analytical approach and empirical techniques yields much more useful results. The resulting empirical model is based on a functional model and therefore easily related to the physical system, yet the assumptions about the system workload can be relaxed because the final form is derived empirically. Anderson and Sargent based their analysis on a queuing model and developed an empirical performance model for workload that could not be successfully fitted by any mathematical distribution function [ANDE72]. Fuller derived an empirical model of the SLTF (Shortest-latency-time-first) drum from an analytical model of simpler drum systems [FULL75A]. In this mode, empirical models provide an important complement to analytical models.

3.4.2 System Profile

A special type of an empirical model is the so-called system profile that provides figures on the utilization of the system resources. A system profile is usually a degenerate form of a performance model in the sense that workload characteristics are not explicitly included as model variables. The system workload shows only in the utilization of individual resources.

A convenient representation of a system profile is the Gantt chart, as shown in figure 3.9. Each horizontal bar represents utilization of a single resource. The overlapped portions indicate the amount of overlap in activities of asynchronously operating components. System profiles are sometimes used for simple quick analysis of the impact of increasing (or decreasing) speed of one or more system components. This method is called profile conversion [BONN69, COCK71, DRUM73]. As an example, consider that the CPU speed would be increased by the factor of 2. The total CPU time needed to complete the same load will decrease by roughly the same factor. The total time for which the other system components are used remains unchanged, but the overlap of their activities with the

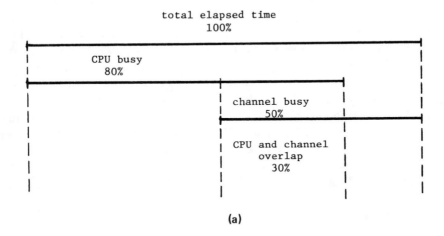

(a)

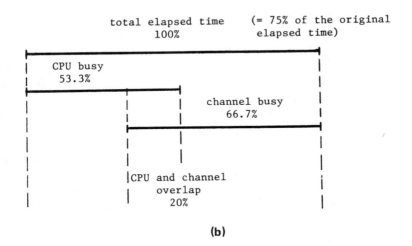

(b)

Figure 3.9. Profile conversion. (a) Original system profile; (b) New system profile for CPU improvement factor of 2.

activities of the CPU will change. Generally, it is assumed that the ratio of the overlapped and the non-overlapped portion remains the same. Thus, the overlapped region is decreased by the CPU improvement factor as it is shown in figure 3.9(b). When two components are changed, the length of their overlapped region is determined by dividing the original region by the greater of the two improvement factors. The improvement in the system performance is measured by the difference in the elapsed time required to process the same load. In the example given in figure 3.9, the improvement is 25% compared to the original system. The rules used in profile conversion are too simplistic; this method should be viewed only as a crude approximation. For a more reliable estimate of the performance improvement, it is necessary to start from a functional model of the system and develop either an analytical model, or use simulation.

BIBLIOGRAPHY

Entries marked with an asterisk (*) are referenced in the text.

ALLE74   Allen, A.O., "Elements of Probability for System Design", *IBM Systems Journal,* Vol. 13, No. 4, 1974, pp. 325–348.

*ANDE72   Anderson, H.A., Sargeant, R.G., "A Statistical Evaluation of the Scheduler of an Experimental Interactive Computing System", *Statistical Computer Performance Evaluation* (Editor: Freiberger, W.), Academic Press, 1972, pp. 73–98.

*ANDJ76   Anderson, J.W., Browne, T.C., "Graph Models of Computer Systems: Application to Performance Evaluation of an Operating System," *Proc. International Symposium on Computer Performance Modeling, Measurement and Evaluation,* March 1976, pp. 166–178.

*BARD71   Bard, Y., "Performance Criteria and Measurement for a Time-Sharing System", *IBM Systems Journal,* Vol. 10, No. 3, 1971, pp. 193–214.

*BASK71   Baskett, F., "The Dependence of Computer System Queues upon Processing Time Distribution and Central Processor Scheduling," *Proc. ACM SIGOPS Third Symposium on Operating System Principles,* October 1971, pp. 109–113.

BASK73A   Baskett, F., Muntz, R.R., "Networks of Queues", *Proc. Seventh Annual Princeton Conference on Information Sciences and Systems,* March 1973.

BASK73B   Baskett, F., "Confidence Intervals for Simulation Results: A Case Study of Buffer Pool Performance", *Proc. Seventh Annual Symposium on the Interface of Computer Science and Statistics,* October 1973, pp. 58–64.

*BASK75   Baskett, F., Chandy, K.M., Muntz, R.R., Palacios, F.G., "Open, Closed, and Mixed Networks of Queues with Different Classes of Customers", *Journal of the ACM,* Vol. 22, No. 2, April 1975, pp. 248–260.

*BHAN75   Bhandarkar, D., "Analysis of Memory Interference in Multiprocessors", *IEEE Transactions on Computers,* Vol. C-24, No. 9, September 1975, pp. 897–908.

*BUZE71   Buzen, J.P., "Analysis of System Bottlenecks Using a Queuing Network Model", *Proc. ACM SIGOPS Workshop on System Performance Evaluation,* April 1971, pp. 82–103.

*BUZE74   Buzen, J.P., Goldberg, P.S., "Guidelines for the Use of Infinite Source Queuing Models in the Analysis of Computer System Performance", *AFIPS Proc. NCC,* 1974, pp. 371–374.

*CHAN75A   Chandy, K.M., Herzog, U., Woo, L., "Parametric Analysis of Queuing Networks", *IBM Journal of Research and Development,* Vol. 19, No. 1, January 1975, pp. 36–42.

*CHAN75B   Chandy, K.M., Herzog, U., Woo, L., "Approximate Analysis of General Queuing Networks", *IBM Journal of Research and Development,* Vol. 19, No. 1, January 1975, pp. 43–49.

*CHAM73   Chamberlin, D.D., Fuller, S.H., Liu, L.Y., "A Page Allocation Strategy for Multiprogramming Systems with Virtual Memory", *IBM Journal of Research and Development,* Vol. 17, No. 1973, pp. 404–412.

*CHEN75   Chen, P.P.S., "Optimal File Allocation in Multi-Level Storage Systems", *AFIPS Proc. NCC,* 1973, pp. 227–282.

*CHIU75   Chiu, W., Dumont, D., Wood, R., "Performance Analysis of a Multiprogrammed Computer System", *IBM Journal of Research and Development,* Vol. 19, No. 3, March 1975, pp. 263–271.

*COCK71   Cockrum, J.S., Crockett, E.D., "Interpreting the Results of a Hardware Systems Monitor", *AFIPS Proc. SJCC,* 1971, pp. 23–38.

*COFF72   Coffman, E.G., Ryan, T.A., "A Study of Storage Partitioning Using a Mathematical Model of Locality", *Communications of the ACM,* Vol. 15, No. 3, March 1972, pp. 185–190.

*COFF73   Coffman, E.G., Denning, P.J., *Operating Systems Theory,* Prentice-Hall, 1973.

*COLL70   Collmeyer, A.J., Shemer, J.E., "Analysis of Retrieval Performance for Selected File Organization Techniques", *AFIPS Proc. FJCC,* 1970, pp. 201–210.

*COOP71   Coop, D.H., "An Analytical Approach to the Measurement, Evaluation, and Prediction of Computer Performance", Ph.D. Diss., Department of Electrical Engineering, University of California, Berkeley, 1971.

COX74   Cox, S.W., "Interpretive Analysis of Computer System Performance", *Proc. Second Annual SIGMETRICS Symposium on Measurement and Evaluation,* September 1974, pp. 140–155.

DECE72   DeCegama, A., "A Methodology for Computer Model Building", *AFIPS Proc. FJCC,* 1972, pp. 301–310.

*DIET73   Diethelm, M.A., "A Method of Evaluating Mass Storage Effects on System Performance", *AFIPS Proc. NCC,* 1973, pp. 69–74.

*DRAP68   Draper, N.R., Smith, H., *Applied Regression Analysis,* John Wiley & Sons, 1968.

*DRUM73   Drummond, M.E., *Evaluation and Measurement Techniques for Digital Computer Systems,* Prentice-Hall, 1973.

*ESTR67A   Estrin, G., Kleinrock, L., "Measures, Models and Measurements for Time-Shared Computer Utilities", *Proc. 22nd ACM National Conference,* 1967, pp. 85–96.

*FULL71   Fuller, S.H., Price, T.G., Wilhelm, N.C., "Measurement and Analysis of a Multiprogrammed Computer System", *Workshop on System Performance Evaluation,* Argonne National Laboratories, June 1971.

*FULL73A   Fuller, S.H., "Performance of an I/O Channel with Multiple Paging Drums", *Proc. First Annual SICME Symposium on Measurement and Evaluation",* February 1973, pp. 13–21.

*FULL75A   Fuller, S.H., Baskett, F., "An Analysis of Drum Storage Units", *Journal of the ACM,* Vol. 22, No. 1, January 1975, pp. 83–105.

*GAVE71   Gaver, D.P., Lewis, P.A.W., "Probability Models for Buffer Storage Allocation Problems", *Journal of the ACM,* Vol. 18, No. 2, April 1971, pp. 186–198.

*GHAN75   Ghanem, M.Z., "Study of Memory Partitioning for Multiprogramming Systems with Virtual Memory", *IBM Journal of Research and Development,* Vol. 19, No. 5, September 1975, pp. 451–457.

*GIAM76   Giammo, T., "Validation of a Computer Performance Model of the Exponential Queuing Network Family," *Proc. International Symposium on Computer Performance Modeling, Measurement and Evaluation,* March 1976, pp. 44–58.

*GRAH73A   Graham, R.M., "Performance Prediction", *Advanced Course on Software Engineering,* Springer-Verlag, 1973, pp. 395–463.

*GRAH73B   Graham, R.M., Clancy, G.J., "A Software Design and Evaluation

System", *Communications of the ACM,* Vol. 16, No. 2, February 1973, pp. 110–116.

GREN72   Grenander, U., Tsao, R.F., "Quantitative Methods for Evaluating Computer System Performance: A Review and Proposals", *Statistical Computer Performance Evaluation* (Editor: Freiberger, W.), Academic Press, 1972, pp. 73–98.

*HANS71   Hansemann, F., Kistler, W., Schulz, H., "Modeling for Computer Center Planning", *IBM Systems Journal,* Vol. 10, No. 4, 1971, pp. 305–324.

*HERZ75   Herzog, U., Woo, L., Chandy, K.M., "Solution of Queuing Problems by a Recursive Technique", *IBM Journal of Research and Development,* Vol. 19, No. 3, May 1975, pp. 295–300.

*HOLT70   Holt, A.W., "An Approach to the Description and Analysis of Dynamic Systems", *Record of the Project MAC Conference on Concurrent Systems and Parallel Computation,* MIT, Cambridge, Massachusetts, June 1970, pp. 3–52.

*HUGP73   Hughes, P.H., Moe, G., "A Structural Approach to Computer Performance Analysis", *AFIPS Proc. NCC,* 1973, pp. 109–120.

KIMB72A   Kimbleton, S.R., "Performance Evaluation—A Structured Approach", *AFIPS Proc. SJCC,* 1972, pp. 411–416.

*KIMB72B   Kimbleton, S.R., "Core Complement Policies for Memory Allocation and Analysis", *AFIPS Proc. FJCC,* 1972, pp. 1155–1162.

*KLEI70A   Kleinrock, L., "A Continum of Time-Sharing Scheduling Algorithms", *AFIPS Proc. SJCC,* 1970, pp. 453–458.

*KLEI75   Kleinrock, L., *Queuing Systems,* Volume I: Theory, John Wiley & Sons, 1975.

*KNUD73   Knudsen, M.T., "PMSL, An Interactive Language for System-Level Description and Analysis of Computer Structures", Ph.D. Diss., Department of Computer Science, Carnegie-Mellon University, April 1973.

*KOBA74A   Kobayashi, H., "Application of the Diffusion Approximation to Queuing Networks I: Equilibrium Queue Distributions", *Journal of the ACM,* Vol. 21, No. 2, pp. 316–328.

*KOBA74B   Kobayashi, H., "Application of the Diffusion Approximation to Queuing Networks II: Nonequilibrium Distributions and Applications to Computer Modeling", *Journal of the ACM,* Vol. 21, No. 3, pp. 459–469.

*LASS72   Lassettre, E.R., Scherr, A.L., "Modeling the Performance of the OS/360 Time-Sharing Option (TSO)", *Statistical Computer Performance Evaluation,* Academic Press, 1972, pp. 57–72.

*MCKI69   McKinney, J.M., "A Survey of Analytical Time-Sharing Models", *Computing Surveys,* Vol. 1, No. 2, June 1969, pp. 105–116.

*NUTT72   Nutt, G.J., "Evaluation Nets for Computer System Performance",
          AFIPS Proc. FJCC, 1972, pp. 279–286.
NUTT73   Nutt, G.J., "The Computer System Representation Problem",
          *Proc. ACM SIGSIM Symposium on the Simulation of Computer
          Systems,* June 1973, pp. 145–149.
*PRIC72   Price, T.G., "An Analysis of Central Processor Scheduling in
          Multiprogrammed Computer Systems", *Technical Report No. 57,*
          Digital Systems Laboratory, Stanford University, Stanford, Cali-
          fornia, October 1972.
*RAMA73   Ramachandani, C., "On the Computation Rate of Asynchronous
          Computation Systems", *Proc. Seventh Annual Princeton Con-
          ference on Information Sciences and Systems,* March 1973.
*REIS75   Reiser, M., Kobayashi, H., "Queuing Networks with Multiple
          Closed Chains: Theory and Computational Algorithms", *IBM
          Journal of Research and Development,* Vol. 19, No. 3, May 1975,
          pp. 283–294.
*REIS76   Reiser, M., Kobayashi, H., "On the Convolution Algorithm for
          Separable Queuing Networks," *Proc. International Symposium on
          Computer Performance Modeling, Measurement and Evaluation,*
          March 1976, pp. 109–117.
*SALT74   Saltzer, J.H., "A Simple Linear Model of Demand Paging Perfor-
          mance", *Communications of the ACM,* Vol. 17, No. 4, April
          1974, pp. 181–186.
*SAST75   Sastry, K.V., Kain, R.Y., "On the Performance of Certain Multi-
          processor Computer Organizations", *IEEE Transactions on Com-
          puters,* Vol. C-24, No. 11, November 1975, pp. 1066–1074.
*SAUE75   Sauer, C.H., Chandy, K.M., "Approximate Analysis of Central
          Server Models", *IBM Journal on Research and Development,* Vol.
          19, No. 3, May 1975, pp. 301–313.
*SEKI72   Sekino, A., "Performance Evaluation of Multiprogrammed Time-
          Shared Computer Systems", *Technical Report MAC TR-103,*
          MIT, Cambridge, Massachusetts, September 1972.
*SEKI73   Sekino, A., "Throughput Analysis of Multiprogrammed Virtual-
          Memory Computer Systems", *Proc. First Annual SICME Sympo-
          sium on Measurement and Evaluation,* February 1973, pp. 47–53.
*SHEM69   Shemer, J.E., Heying, D.W., "Performance Modeling and Empiri-
          cal Measurements in a System Designed for Batch and Time-
          Sharing Users", *AFIPS Proc. FJCC,* 1969, pp. 17–26.
*SIEW74   Siewiorek, D., "Introducing PMS", *Computer,* Vol. 7, No. 12,
          December 1974, pp. 42–44.
*SMIT73   Smith, A.J., "A Performance Analysis of Multiple Channel Con-

trollers", *Proc. First Annual SICME Symposium on Measurement and Evaluation,* February 1973, pp. 37–46.

STRA71   Strauss, J.C., "A Simple Thruput and Response Model of EXEC 8 Under Swapping Saturation", *AFIPS Proc. FJCC,* 1971, pp. 39–49.

*TEOR72   Teorey, T.J., "Properties of Disk Scheduling Policies in Multi-programmed Computer Systems", *AFIPS Proc. FJCC,* 1972, pp. 1–11.

*TSAO72   Tsao, R.F., Margolin, B.H., "A Multi-Factor Paging Experiment: II. Statistical Methodology", *Statistical Computer Performance Evaluation,* Academic Press, 1972, pp. 135–158.

*WALD73   Waldbaum, G., "Evaluating Computing System Changes by Means of Regression Models", *Proc. First Annual SICME Symposium on Measurement and Evaluation,* February 1973, pp. 127–135.

*WATS71   Watson, R., "Computer Performance Analysis: Applications of Accounting Data", *Report R-573-NASA/PR,* Rand Corporation, Santa Monica, California, May 1971.

*WILH73   Wilhelm, N.C., "A General Model for the Performance of Disk Systems", *Technical Report No. 63,* Digital Systems Laboratory, Stanford University, Stanford, California, August 1973.

Chapter 4

Workload Models

Performance is a reaction of a system to a specific workload. It is, therefore, essential that the right workload is used when evaluating the system and that the workload characterization is sufficiently representative to account for all significant factors.

A workload model serves as a drive workload of a real computer system during performance measurement experiments or as an input to a model of the evaluated system. The purpose of using workload models is to:

- Provide a representative workload for comparative performance evaluation of different systems.
- Provide a controllable reproducible environment for experimental performance optimization studies.
- Reduce the quantity of data that have to be analyzed.
- Present the system workload in a form required by a system model.

Alternate choices in system configuration and algorithms and the effect of different control parameters must be evaluated for the same workload. Generally, only one alternative can be examined at a time, thus requiring that the workload used as the input to the system during evaluation be reproducible.

The real system workload, that is, the workload generated by the user community in the normal production environment, is generally irreproducible in its exact composition. However, if the statistical properties of the system workload do not change with time, the workload is statistically reproducible. The real workload can be used to drive the system during evaluation experiments, but the measurement intervals must be sufficiently long, and it is necessary to collect and analyze large amounts of data to ensure that the statistics are correct. The minimum measurement interval may range from minutes or hours if the system workload does not change with the time of day, to weeks or months if the workload exhibits significant changes with such periodicity. System workload may remain stationary for quite long periods of time, but in general, its characteristics change slowly as the user community changes, new applications are added and the old discontinued. In addition to that, the user community tends to adapt to system changes, and as the users change their habits, the workload characteristics change too. Thus, in a long term, the real workload is not reproducible. Finally, the experimenter has no control over the system input and it is thus difficult to ascertain the effects of different workload characteristics on system performance. For these reasons, it is preferable, and sometimes necessary, to construct a special drive workload even when it is physically feasible to measure the system under its real workload.

System workload was said to be characterized by demands for system resources (system components). Ideally, a workload model should have the same characteristics as the real workload. Since workload characterization is still not sufficiently understood, representativeness of a workload model is frequently measured only by the resulting system performance [FERR72A], that is, a workload model is accepted as being representative of the real workload if its application results in the same steady state performance. This approach may be sufficient for many comparison studies and performance tuning projects, but the lack of proper understanding of workload characteristics is a serious obstacle when the goal is to predict performance effects of system changes and design alternatives. Extensive empirical studies of programs may reveal many interesting properties that should be considered during the initial system design [BATS70, BRUN75, KNUT71]. In addition, it is necessary to study the habits of system users. Performance effects of certain system changes measured against a once representative workload model may be positive, yet in reality, the users may react to these changes in such a way that the over-all effect will be negative. This problem becomes particularly evident when computer services are used for the first time. The true behavior of the eventual users may be quite different from the behavior assumed for the purpose of system selection or design [WARN72].[1]

---

[1] A fitting description of the present state of the art is the paraphrased quote used by Ferrari: "Blessed is he who found his computer's workload. Let him ask no other blessedness." [FERR72A].

A system that is too carefully tuned to a specific projected workload might not meet the performance objectives if the real workload turns out to have different characteristics. It is thus necessary to have a means of examining performance in the light of different workloads. Flexibility and controllability of workload characteristics is an important property of a workload model.

Different types of workload models have been in use. The rest of this chapter examines individual types in detail.

4.1 INSTRUCTION MIX

Instruction mix specifies the relative usage of different types of instructions in a particular application. Since each instruction may require different time to execute, performance (instruction execution rate) of an instruction set processor must be evaluated with respect to the requested instruction mix.

Instruction mix is used in two main areas:

1. selection of computer hardware, and
2. design of new processors.

In the first case, the "typical" instruction mix for the class of applications planned for the system must be defined such that it can be used across a wide range of different instruction sets. That is, a typical instruction mix specifies frequencies of different functions (add, multiply, jump, logical operations), rather than actual instructions that perform these functions. The most frequently used instruction mix is the Gibson mix [GIBS70], which could be classified as a "general purpose" mix. Instruction mixes for a number of different applications are presented in [CORS70].

Instruction mix, however, depends on many factors that are difficult to account for, such as the number of operands per instruction or different addressing modes. Due to these factors, the number of instructions needed to code the same task on different machines may vary significantly. Also, the instruction mix is dependent on the programming language in which the application is coded, the translator of this language, and finally, the programmer. The significance of these factors was demonstrated by Lunde [LUND74].[2] However,

---

[2] This particular study concentrated on analysis of one specific instruction set

there is one specific area where one need not be concerned about the above-discussed factors, and that is selection or design of an instruction set processor emulator for already existing application programs [SALI73].

4.2 BENCHMARKS

Benchmark is defined as "a point of reference from which measurements can be made" [SIPP72]. A benchmark can be an instruction, a special program or a sequence of calls to selected software components. In most cases, however, the term benchmark is used to mean a job or a set of jobs that represents a typical workload of the evaluated system. Benchmarks play the role of a drive workload in the real system, both for the purpose of comparative evaluation of different systems and performance optimization. A good benchmark must exercise all system functions (job scheduling, file management, I/O support, language processors, etc.) in a manner in which these functions are used or are expected to be used in the actual production environment.

A benchmark representative of the current system workload can be assembled from already existing programs. Jobs to be included in the benchmark may be selected by random sampling of the job stream [SHOP70]. This method does not require an explicit knowledge of characteristics of individual jobs, but it is then difficult to determine how many of these randomly-selected jobs must be included in the benchmark.

The real system workload generally consists of several classes of applications (scientific problems, payroll, file update, etc.). A benchmark, or as sometimes called, a benchmark mix, can be constructed as a properly weighted mix of jobs representative of each class [JOSL65]. However, demand characteristics of jobs in the same application class may vary significantly, while demand characteristics of jobs performing different functions may greatly overlap.

The most rigorous approach rests on partitioning jobs into classes according to their characteristics. The job with characteristics closest to the typical characteristics for its class is selected to represent the

---

processor (PDP–10). Eight different applications were coded in four different higher-level languages (ALGOL, BASIC, BLISS, and FORTRAN); one application was coded by three different programmers.

class in the benchmark. A selected job is assigned weight proportional to the percentage of workload that falls into that same category. Partitioning of jobs according to their true characteristics can be accomplished by cluster analysis. A clustering algorithm assigns jobs to a predetermined number of groups called clusters such that the differences between members of the same cluster are small compared to differences between numbers of different clusters. The process and the results of clustering jobs into a varying number of groups were described in [HUNT71].

A benchmark constructed from real jobs is apt to be system dependent. In general, such benchmark is not directly usable as a drive workload of a different system. A considerable conversion effort may be necessary to create a benchmark for several different systems. An instructive case study of a benchmark-based evaluation of several systems from different vendors[3] was published by Strauss [STRA72].

To evaluate system performance for projected workload, special programs may have to be written for the benchmark. In such case, a benchmark also provides a measure of the effort needed to program new applications and interface them with the system. While this is a possible advantage of using 'real' jobs for a benchmark, this approach has a number of disadvantages. It is not always possible to construct a drive workload from jobs obtained from the real job stream, either because of security reasons, or because execution of real jobs causes permanent changes in the system (e.g., file update). Also, it is often difficult to find a real job that fits the typical characteristics of a particular class.

4.3 SYNTHETIC BENCHMARKS

The system workload can be viewed as a sequence of demands for system services that is mapped by the system software into a sequence of demands for system resources. For most evaluation purposes, knowledge of the resource demands is all that is necessary; the actual code is not important.

A synthetic benchmark simulates usage of system resources as prescribed by characteristics of the modeled workload, but it does no

---

[3] The benchmark conversion effort was undertaken by the competing vendors.

"useful" work. A synthetic benchmark can be constructed either from the resource demands or the service demands [MORG73]. The latter approach makes the synthetic benchmark independent of the system configuration and the operating system. A synthetic benchmark based on service demands can thus be used for comparative evaluation of different systems. The structure of resource demands or service demands form the framework of a synthetic benchmark. These demands can be obtained by measuring the system under its real workload, estimated for projected workload, or designed to test a system under workload that represents limiting or unusual conditions.

The demand structure can be used directly as an input to a system simulator. If a synthetic benchmark is to be used as a drive workload of the real system, the demand structure has to be converted into executable programs, called synthetic jobs. A synthetic job can simulate CPU requirements by controlled looping,[4] I/O requirements by reading and writing a scratch file. The actual characteristics of a synthetic job can be changed through a set of control parameters.[5]

A synthetic benchmark can be obtained as a mix of synthetic jobs where individual jobs are assigned different values for the control parameters [SREE74]. Generation of such mix can be automized to produce benchmarks for different workloads and even for different systems [KERG73].

4.4 TRACE

A trace is a record of selected events that preserves the exact sequence in which these events occurred in the system. An event can be defined as a change in the system state. An event can be a job initiation, a job being assigned the CPU, start and end of an I/O operation, execution of an instruction. A trace is used as a drive workload for a simulation model, especially for analysis where the sequence pattern is important. A trace can be classified as instruction

---

[4] As pointed out in [BARB75], one must be careful as to how this loop is implemented. An optimizing compiler may effectively remove a loop that does not do anything.
[5] A good example of a parametrized synthetic job is Buchholz's synthetic job simulating a file updating process [BUCH69].

trace [WIND73, LUND74], memory address trace [MATT70], jump
trace [BAIL72], or resource allocation trace [CHEG69].

A trace is prepared either from the system natural workload or
from a representative benchmark mix. A trace can be acquired either
by hardware or software monitors (see Chapter 6). Software implemented tracing of such events as instruction executions or memory
references must be done interpretatively. The CPU then appears to
operate many times slower than in its normal mode. Since the
processing speeds of other system resources remain unchanged, interactions of these resources and the CPU become time-skewed. Thus, a
trace has to be used cautiously, since for some purposes it may not
be representative.

4.5 PROBABILISTIC WORKLOAD MODELS

Probabilistic workload models are used in analytical studies and in
simulation. Resource demands are assumed to be random variables
and the workload is described by their distributions. The real distributions are frequently approximated by the exponential distribution,
since the properties of this distribution significantly simplify mathematical analysis of systems. Other used distributions are the geo-
metric distribution, the hyperexponential distribution and the Erlang
distribution. In general, workload characteristics are difficult to fit
by a mathematically simple distribution [ANDE72, FULL71], but
workload models based on such distributions were shown to yield
performance sufficiently close to the performance obtained from the
real system.

4.6 INTERACTIVE SYSTEM DRIVERS

Workload of an interactive system is heavily influenced by users'
characteristics: think time, type time, user generated interrupts. A
drive workload for an interactive system must represent the users as
well as their programs. An interactive system driver is not a workload
model, but its generator. It consists of a model of the user interface
and a model of users' processing requirements. The model of the user
interface intercepts all system operations directed to users' terminals
and simulates the appropriate action. This component can be implemented either internally as a program that runs on the tested system

[FOGE72, DEME69], or externally in a separate hardware processor [GREE68, SCHW72]. An internal driver reduces the amount of resources available for processing of users' jobs. This problem will be discussed in more detail in connection with internal software monitors (Chapter 6). The model of the user processing requirements consists of benchmarks executed from the simulated terminals. The benchmarks are either synthetic or constructed from the real system commands and input data. The latter form of a terminal benchmark is called a script. It is also possible to use a probabilistic model of user processing requirements, that is, the characteristics of terminal requests can be drawn automatically from probability distributions.

BIBLIOGRAPHY

Entries marked with an asterisk (*) are referenced in the text.

*ANDE72   Anderson, H.A., Sargeant, R.G., "A Statistical Evaluation of the Scheduler of an Experimental Interactive Computing System", *Statistical Computer Performance Evaluation,* Academic Press, 1972, pp. 73–98.

*BAIL72   Bailliu, G., Ferrari, D., "A Method to Model Microprograms and Analyze Their Behavior", *COMPCON 72 (Digest of Papers),* Sixth Annual IEEE Comp. Soc. Internat'l Conf., 1972, pp. 115–118.

*BARB75   Barber, E.O., Asphjell, A., Dispen, A., "Benchmark Construction", *ACM SIGMETRICS Performance Evaluation Review,* Vol. 4, No. 4, October 1975, pp. 3–14.

*BATS70   Batson, A., Shy-Ming, J., Wood, D.C., "Measurement of Segment Size", *Communications of the ACM,* Vol. 13, No. 3, March 1970, pp. 155–159.

*BRUN75   Brundage, R.E., Batson, A.P., "Computational Processor Demands of Algol-60 Programs", *Proc. Fifth SIGOPS Symposium on Operating Systems Principles,* November 1975, pp. 161–168.

*BUCH69   Buchholz, W., "A Synthetic Job for Measuring System Performance", *IBM Systems Journal,* Vol. 8, No. 4, 1969, pp. 309–318.

*CHEG69   Cheng, P.S., "Trace Driven System Modeling", *IBM Systems Journal,* Vol. 8, No. 4, 1969, pp. 280–289.

*CORS70   Corsiglia, J., "Matching Computers to the Job—First Step Toward Selection", *Data Processing Magazine,* December 1970, pp. 23–27.

*DEME69   DeMeis, W.M., Weizer, N., "Measurement and Analysis of a Demand Paging Time-Sharing System", *Proc. 24th ACM National Conference,* 1969, pp. 201–216.

*FERR72A   Ferrari, D., "Workload Characterization and Selection in Computer Performance Measurement", *Computer,* July/August 1972, pp. 18–24.

*FOGE72   Fogel, M., Winograd, J., "EINSTEIN: An Internal Driver in a Time-Sharing Environment", *ACM SIGOPS Operating Systems Review,* October 1972, pp. 6–14.

FOST71   Foster, C.C., Gonter, R.H., "Conditional Interpretation of Operation Codes", *IEEE Transactions on Computers,* Vol. C-20, No. 1, January 1971, pp. 108–111.

*FULL71   Fuller, S.H., Price, T.G., Wilhelm, N.C., "Measurement and Analysis of a Multiprogrammed Computer Systems", *Workshop on System Performance Evaluation,* Argonne National Laboratories, June 1971.

*GIBS70   Gibson, J.C., "The Gibson Mix", IBM TR 00.2043, June 1970.

*GREE68   Greenbaum, H.J., "A Simulator of Multiple Interactive Users to Drive a Time Shared Computer System", *Technical Report No. 58,* Project MAC, MIT, Cambridge, Massachusetts, 1968.

*HUNT71   Hunt, E., Diehr, G., Garnatz, D., "Who are the users?–An Analysis of Computer Use in a University Computer Center", *AFIPS Proc. SJCC,* 1971, pp. 231–238.

*JOSL65   Joslin, E.O., "Application Benchmarks: The Key to Meaningful Computer Evaluation", *Proc. 20th ACM National Conference,* 1965, pp. 27–37.

*KERG73   Kernighan, B.W., Hamilton, P.A., "Synthetically Generated Performance Test Loads for Operating Systems", *Proc. First Annual SICME Symposium on Measurement and Evaluation,* February 1973, pp. 121–126.

KERN72   Kerner, H., Kuemmerle, K., "Performance Measures, Definitions and Metric", *Proc. Sixth Annual Princeton Conference on Information Sciences and Systems,* March 1972, pp. 213–217.

KNIG66   Knight, K.E., "Changes in Computer Performance: A Historical Review", *Datamation,* Vol. 12, No. 9, September 1966, pp. 40–54.

*KNUT71   Knuth, D.E., "An Empirical Study of FORTRAN Programs", *Software–Practice and Experience,* Vol. 1, No. 1, 1971, pp. 105–133.

*LUND74   Lunde, A., "Evaluation of Instruction Set Processor Architecture by Program Tracing", Ph.D. thesis, Department of Computer Science, Carnegie-Mellon University, July 1974.

*MATT70   Mattson, R.L., Gecsei, J., Slutz, D.R., Traiger, I.L., "Evaluation

Techniques for Storage Hierarchies", *IBM Systems Journal,* Vol. 9, No. 2, 1970, pp. 78–117.

*MORG73   Morgan, D.E., Campbell, J.A., "An Answer to a User's Plea?" *Proc. First Annual SICME Symposium on Measurement and Evaluation,* February 1973, pp. 112–120.

*SALI73   Salisbury, A.B., "The Evaluation of Microprogram Implemented Emulators", *Technical Report No. 60,* Digital Systems Laboratory, Stanford, California, July 1973.

SCHA75   Schatroff, M., Tillman, C.C., "Design of Experiments in Simulator Validation", *IBM Journal on Research and Development,* Vol. 19, No. 3, May 1975, pp. 252–262.

*SCHW72   Schwemm, R.E., "Experience Gained in the Development and Use of TSS", *AFIPS Proc. SJCC,* 1972, pp. 559–569.

SHET74   Shetler, A.C., "Controlled Testing for Computer Performance Evaluation", *AFIPS Proc. NCC,* 1974, pp. 693–699.

*SHOP70   Shope, W.L., Kashmarack, K.L., Inghram, J.W., Decker, W.F., "System Performance Study", *Proc. SHARE XXXIV,* Vol. 1, March 1970, pp. 439–530.

*SIPP72   Sippl, C.J., Sippl, C.P., *Computer Dictionary and Handbook,* Howard W. Sams & Co., 1972.

*SREE74   Sreenivasan, K., Kleiman, A.J., "On the Construction of a Representable Synthetic Workload", *Communications of the ACM,* Vol. 17, No. 3, March 1974, pp. 127–133.

*STRA72   Strauss, J.C., "A Benchmark Study", *AFIPS Proc. FJCC,* 1972, pp. 1225–1233.

SVOB74A   Svobodova, L., "Computer System Performance Measurement: Instruction Set Processor Level and Microcode Level", *Technical Report No. 66,* Digital Systems Laboratory, Stanford University, Stanford, California, June 1974.

*SYMS74   Syms, G.H., "Benchmarked Comparison of Terminal Support Systems for IBM 360 Computers", *Performance Evaluation Review,* Vol. 2, No. 3, September 1974, pp. 6–34.

*WARN72   Warner, D.C., "System Performance and Evaluation–Past, Present, and Future", *AFIPS Proc. FJCC,* 1972, pp. 959–964.

*WIND73   Winder, R.O., "A Data Base for Computer Performance Evaluation", *Computer,* Vol. 6, No. 3, March 1973, pp. 25–29.

*WOOD71   Wood, D.C., Forman, E.H., "Throughput Measurements Using a Synthetic Job Stream", *AFIPS Proc. FJCC,* 1971, pp. 51–55.

Chapter 5

Simulation

The technique of simulation can be viewed as a combination of modeling and measurement. The simulation process requires a model of the system, a model of the workload, and a simulator. A simulator is a mechanism that simulates system behavior as specified by the functional model of the system and the workload model and collects the necessary data required for performance analysis. The performance model of the system is derived empirically, as in the case of measuring the real system.

For mathematical analysis, the system as well as the system workload must be greatly simplified. Simulation can examine computer systems in much more detail. Simulation is used as an extension of mathematical analysis to derive empirical results where a closed form expression cannot be obtained [FULL75, LAVE75B], or to validate analytical models [FULL73A, KOBA74A, SMIT73, WILH73]. A simulation model can include factors that are very difficult to incorporate into an analytical model, such as dynamic memory allocation or various system overhead. Also, the workload does not have to be described by stationary probability distributions, though it is a frequently used approach. Since programs' memory referencing patterns are very difficult to describe stochastically, studies of paging strategies and memory organizations generally require a simulation experiment [CHU72, HATF72, HEND74, KAPL73, MATT70].

Besides studies that, similar to analytical studies, help to build the body of theory, simulation has many direct practical applications. Essentially, simulation is the only method for estimating performance of new designs and new configurations before actually implementing them. Simulation is used to determine possible improvements in performance of existing systems [BARK69, BEIL72, GOTL73, NOE72], for evaluation of computer networks [KLEI70B], selection of new computer systems [CANN68], and as a design tool [CAPL74, FIKE73, HAKO73, HUTC73, MURJ70, NOLT73].

For performance analysis, a simulator must only simulate those events that change the system state. Such simulators are called discrete event simulators. A discrete event simulator maintains a simulation clock that is advanced after each change of the system state by a variable amount corresponding to the real time that must elapse before the next change takes place. This mechanism makes the simulation process independent of the speed of the computer system on which the simulator runs.

The level of detail included in a simulation model has to be considered extremely carefully. Simulation based on too few details might not yield reliable results. As more details are included, simulation becomes more costly, both in development and use. Theory and Merten compared the relative cost of simulation on different levels [TEOR73]. Provided that the average time between subsequent changes in the state of the real system is much longer than the time it takes to simulate a change of state, simulation takes considerably less time than the equivalent amount of processing in the real system. Thus a gross functional model similar to models studied analytically may be simulated 10 to 50 times faster than real time.[1] However, a more detailed functional model needed for a design of an operating system may be up to 20 times slower than real time. Finally, simulation on the ISP level is usually more than 20 times slower. These numbers depend, of course, on the implementation of the simulator and the computer system on which the simulator runs. Even if the cost of computer use is not an important consideration, detailed simulation may turn out to be unfeasible because it cannot be completed in reasonable time. Finally, too many details sometimes generate "noise," a large variance that makes certain general aspects of the system's behavior less easily identifiable.

Problems encountered in large-scale simulation are manifold [BELT72B]. Most of these problems must be resolved before building a simulator. A simulator is only a tool that facilitates certain experiments. The characteristics of the desired experiments must be projected into the design of a simulator. The simulator must be sufficiently flexible to allow testing of all interesting design alterna-

---

[1] This factor can be even more dramatic. For example, execution of 650 jobs requiring fourteen hours of real time was simulated in one minute [BEIL72].

tives and conditions such as scheduling algorithms, system configurations, workload composition, or a combination of these. A very important function of a simulator is collecting statistics about the simulated system. This function is similar to that performed by monitors in a real system. In a simulator, this can be accomplished directly by the same mechanism that schedules and processes events. Finally, it is necessary to select a suitable representation for the system workload.

5.1 STOCHASTIC SIMULATION

Computer system simulators can be classified according to the representation of the system workload. In stochastic (Monte Carlo) simulation, the workload is described by probability distributions. The demands for the resources of the simulated system model are generated as random samples from specified distributions. Thus, a good random number generator is essential to stochastic simulation.

Computer-based random number generators produce uniformly distributed numbers. Random samples from other distributions can be obtained only indirectly, using random numbers uniformly distributed between 0 and 1 [KNUT69, FULL75B]. The target distributions can be described mathematically or presented in a tabular form.

An instructive example of a simple stochastic simulator based on a queuing model is McDougall's BASYS simulator [MCDO70]. The BASYS simulator simulates a multiprogramming system consisting of a CPU, a main memory, and a movable-head disk. The functional model of this system is outlined in figure 5.1. The workload is specified by distributions of five characteristics:

1. Job interarrival time
2. Job main memory requirements
3. Job CPU time requirements
4. Number of I/O requests made by a given job
5. Length of I/O records manipulated by a given job

The simulator generates jobs with interarrival times and demand characteristics as random quantities from appropriate distributions. The movement of a job through the system is represented by a

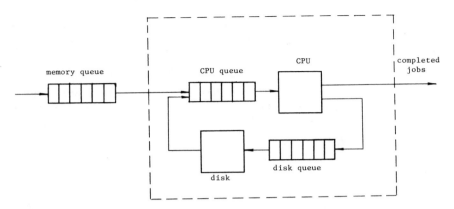

Figure 5.1. Functional model for simulating a multiprogramming system.

sequence of events that mark the beginning and the end of different job's activities. When an event marking the beginning of a job's activity occurs, the time of occurrence of the next event caused by the same job can be calculated from job's characteristics. The simulator maintains a chronological list of these future events for all concurrent jobs. The simulation clock is simply advanced to the time of the next scheduled event.

The statistics collected by the simulator must represent the steady state performance of the simulated system. However, the simulator cannot start instantly in the steady state. Therefore, the collection of statistics should not start immediately, but only after the simulated system is brought into the steady state. The accuracy of the results depends on the number of observations collected for each measured variable. Provided that successive observations of a measured variable are independent and identically distributed, confidence intervals for the statistical estimate of this variable can be determined by classical statistical methods. However, successive observations of many interesting variables are not statistically independent (e.g., wait time in a processor's queue), necessitating a different approach. One solution is to use time series analysis of the successive observations of the measured variable [FISH67]. Another approach is to repeat each experiment many times and count each experiment as a single observation. Independent runs of a simulation experiment produce independent identically distributed observations.[2] Of course, for each run, the simulated system must first be brought into the steady state.

The problem of estimating accuracy of simulation results is substantially simplified if the simulated system has at least one regeneration point. A regeneration point is a state of the system in which the system's future behavior is completely independent of its past behavior and to which the system repeatedly returns. Each cycle, that is, a period between successive returns to the regeneration point, can be viewed as a single observation; these observations are again independent and identically distributed. In addition, data collection can be started any time the system reaches the regeneration point. This method was introduced by Crane and Iglehart [CRAN74A, CRAN74B, CRAN75][3] and was found to be applicable to many computer system problems [BASK73B, LAVE75B].

5.2 TRACE DRIVEN SIMULATION

The mechanism used in the stochastic simulator generates resource demands that drive the system model as random numbers from a set of distributions. Alternatively, the workload of a simulated computer system can be represented directly by a deterministic sequence of resource demands. Such sequences can be built artificially or extracted from an event trace obtained by measuring an existing computer system. A trace, as discussed in Chapter 4, is a time-ordered record of important events that occurred while a particular computer system was processing its natural workload or some selected benchmark. A trace driven simulator is an excellent tool for tuning the system [GOTL73]. Trace driven simulation can be used for studying performance of different system configurations [CHEG69], for analysis of different resource management strategies

---

[2] The computer methods for random number generation are deterministic. The sequences of numbers produced by a random number generator can be repeated by starting the generator from the same point. Reproducibility, as it was discussed in Chapter 4, is an important property of a workload model. In this case, however, the sequences used in different runs must be different; for each run, the generator must be started from a different point.

[3] A tutorial presentation of this method can be found in [LAVE75A].

[SCHA75, SHER72], and also for performance evaluation of new designs [MURJ70].

The main advantage of trace driven simulation is the high level of detail possible in the workload description, such that correlation and interference of resource demands encountered in the real system can be preserved with sufficient accuracy.[4] Thus, trace driven simulators can be used for very detailed analysis, especially where the exact pattern of requests is important. The best representatives of this category are simulators dealing with memory reference patterns [CHU72, HATF72, HEND74, KAPL73, MATT70].

Trace driven simulation also has its problems. To study resource management strategies, it is necessary to know the characteristics of individual jobs. In a trace, these characteristics are often mixed with the effects of multiprogramming and their separation may be difficult. A possible solution is to trace individual jobs as they are run sequentially [CHEG69]. However, the multiprogramming effects must be measured for the validation purpose. Thus, the jobs traced in the sequential mode must also be run in the multiprogramming mode.

Validation of a trace driven simulator is reduced to comparison of the used trace with the output of the simulator. Beilner and Waldbaum describe a statistical methodology for validating a trace driven simulator [BEIL72]. First, the simulator is calibrated for one specific trace. Calibration consists of modifying the structure and tuning various parameters of the simulator such that the results of simulation match the trace. Calibration is performed in two directions:

1. Balancing the simulator such that the processing of jobs of different types is simulated with the same accuracy (linear regression of errors versus job characteristics).
2. Minimizing the over-all error (linear regression of errors versus calibration parameters of the simulator).

The danger of this approach is overtuning a simulator. That is, a simulator may turn out to "fit" only one specific sequence of jobs.

---

[4] A more detailed account of advantages and problems of trace driven simulation is given in [SHER73].

The validity of a simulation model can be established only by testing the simulator with many different traces that capture all different aspects of the system's workload. Furthermore, a simulator must yield valid results not just for the current version of the system, but for all system variations to be investigated. Confidence in simulation results can be increased by an experiment that tests the simulator for several simple system changes (e.g., different values of system control parameters) [SCHA75].

5.3 SIMULATION TOOLS

Simulation tools consist of simulation languages and specialized simulators. Simulation languages provide the basic mechanism for constructing a discrete event simulator for a general system. The other, a higher level, tool, the specialized simulator, has a substantial built-in knowledge about a specific class of systems; that is, in our case, computer systems.

A simulator can be implemented in any general purpose programming language. However, there exists a number of simulation languages that have built-in facilities for scheduling discrete events and gathering basic statistics. Kay identified three basic families of simulation languages, represented by GASP, GPSS and SIMSCRIPT [KAY72]. The languages of the GASP family are based on a common scientific language (FORTRAN, ALGOL). The special simulation facilities are merely an extension implemented as a set of subroutines. The languages of the GPSS family are block diagram languages. The model of a simulated system is built as a block diagram, different shapes of blocks representing different functions. In the actual program, each block is described by a simple control statement. The simulator supplies all the necessary mechanisms, including data collection facilities. These languages thus facilitate easy transitions from logical designs to executable programs. The languages of the SIMSCRIPT family are the most powerful and flexible simulation languages; however, they require more programming expertise. What can be described by a single GPSS statement requires a special routine in SIMSCRIPT.[5]

---

[5] Graham demonstrates the differences of these two languages on an implementation of the BASYS simulator [GRAH73A]. An ALGOL implementation of a simulator for a similar multiprogramming system is described in [FULL75B].

The selection of language for implementing a computer system simulator is influenced by the purpose and the extent of simulation. While simulation languages provide convenient facilities, they usually require more execution time. Other possibly negative factors are the cost of acquiring the language translator and the time required to learn a new language. A computer system simulator implemented in FORTRAN is a frequent phenomenon [FULL72B, NOE72, NOLT73].

Modeling of special features is sometimes easier in a lower level language. Microprogrammable computers open up the possibility of implementing a simulator directly in microcode. This technique is used mainly on the instruction set processor level, where it is known as emulation. However, this technique is also useful for studying effects of hardware changes. Performance changes due to new hardware components (memories, peripheral devices) can be tested by measuring the existing system where only the interface between the new component and the old hardware is simulated [SVOB76].

A simulator such as BASYS is suitable and sufficient only for studying resource management policies. Scheduling overhead can be included in the model, but, similar to analytical models, hardware characteristics are only implicit. Speed of hardware components must be reflected in the workload specification, that is, instead of working with a description of what has to be done, it is necessary to specify how much of the system resources are required. This amount is, of course, different for different systems. More powerful simulators are necessary for guiding systems reconfiguration and system selection [WINO70]. Several powerful computer system simulators were developed that can simulate and evaluate a great variety of combined hardware and software configurations [CANN68, HUES67]. Some of these simulators have an extensive library of models of different hardware and software components [IHRE67, SEAM69]. The input to the simulator is a description of the hardware configuration, the software configuration, and the workload. The workload of the simulated system is represented by synthetic jobs; each job consists of a sequence of demands for system resources or services described in a special macrolanguage. From the input information and the information stored in the library, the simulator builds a functional model of the simulated system and runs this model with the specified workload. Of course, the system components specified in the input must be "known" to the simulator. More flexible computer system simulators include facilities for describing arbitrary hardware components and software functions to be included in the system model [DEWA72, NIEL69, KOSY73].

Despite the associated problems, simulation is the most general, most flexible, and most powerful technique for studying and predicting system performance. A simulation model, unlike analytical models, can be easily assembled from separate models of individual components. Each system component can be simulated on a different level of detail, as long as the interface between the components is simulated properly [TEOR73]. In fact, some components may be modeled analytically, while others are simulated.

This is a real asset in system design and development. In a top-down approach, a system is first designed and simulated on a very high level. As more information becomes available, individual system components are progressively replaced by more and more detailed and accurate models [CAPL74, GRAH73B]. Alternative designs of system components can be examined on a component model as well as within the whole system. Once it is shown that a component meets performance criteria and interfaces properly with the rest of the system, it can again be replaced by a gross model that simulates only the interface, thus keeping the cost of simulation within limits. The feasibility of design can be constantly tested as the system evolves and the system performance can be predicted with good accuracy before the system is completely implemented. In fact, in the case of a software system, design and simulation can merge such that the final model becomes the new system [GRAH73B].

BIBLIOGRAPHY

Entries marked with an asterisk (*) are referenced in the text.

*BARK69   Barker, P.E., Watson, H.K., "Calibrating the Simulation Model of the IBM/360 Time-sharing System", *Proc. Third Conference on Application of Simulation,* 1969, pp. 130–137.

*BASK73B   Baskett, F., "Confidence Intervals for Simulation Results: A Case Study of Buffer Pool Performance", *Proc. Seventh Annual Symposium on the Interface of Computer Science and Statistics,* October 1973, pp. 58–64.

*BEIL72   Beilner, H., Waldbaum, G., "Statistical Methodology for Calibrating a Trace-Driven Simulator for a Batch Computer System", in *Statistical Computer Performance Evaluation,* (Editor: Freiberger, W.), Academic Press, 1972, pp. 423–459.

*BELT72B   Bell, T.E., "Objectives and Problems in Simulating Computers", *AFIPS Proc. FJCC,* 1972, pp. 287–297.

*BOWD73   Bowdon, E.K., Mamrak, S.A., Salz, F.R., "Simulation–A Tool for Performance Evaluation in Network Computers", *AFIPS Proc. NCC,* 1973, pp. 121–131.

*CANN68   Canning, R.G., "Data Processing Planning via Simulation", *EDP Analysis,* Vol. 6, No. 4, April 1968, pp. 1–13.

*CAPL74   Caplener, H.D., Janku, J.A., "Top-Down Approach to LSI System Design", *Computer Design,* Vol. 13, No. 8, August 1974, pp. 143–148.

*CHEG69   Cheng, P.S., "Trace Driven System Modeling", *IBM Systems Journal,* Vol. 8, No. 4, 1969, pp. 280–289.

*CHU72   Chu, W.W., Opderbeck, H., "The Page Fault Frequency (PFF) Replacement Algorithm", *AFIPS Proc. FJCC,* 1972, pp. 597–609.

*CRAN74A   Crane, M.A., Iglehart, D.L., "Simulating Stable Stochastic Systems, I: General Multiserver Queues", *Journal of the ACM,* Vol. 21, No. 1, January 1974, pp. 103–113.

*CRAN74B   Crane, M.A., Iglehart, D.L., "Simulating Stable Stochastic Systems, II: Markov Chains", *Journal of the ACM,* Vol. 21, No. 2, April 1974, pp. 114–123.

*CRAN75   Crane, M.A., Iglehart, D.L., "Simulating Stable Stochastic Systems, III: Regenerative Processes and Discrete Event Simulations", *Operations Research,* Vol. 23, No. 1, 1975, p. 33.

*DEWA72   Dewan, P.B., Donaghey, C.E., Wyatt, J.B., "OSSL–A Specialized Language for Simulating Computer Systems", *AFIPS Proc. SJCC,* 1972, pp. 799–814.

*FIKE73   Fike, J.L., Szygenda, S.A., "Techniques and Moduls for Element Specification in a Time-Delay Logic Simulator", *Proc. ACM SIG-SIM Symposium on the Simulation of Computer Systems,* June 1973, pp. 277–287.

*FISH67   Fishman, G.S., Kiviat, P.J., "The Analysis of Simulation Generated Time Series", *Management Science,* Vol. 13, 1967, pp. 525–557.

*FULL72B   Fuller, S.H., "A Simulator for Computer Systems with Storage Units Having Rotational Delays", *Technical Note No. 16,* Digital Systems Laboratory, Stanford University, Stanford, California, August 1972.

*FULL73A   Fuller, S.H., "Performance of an I/O Channel with Multiple Paging Drums", *Proc. First Annual SICME Symposium on Measurement and Evaluation,* February 1973, pp. 13–21.

*FULL73B   Fuller, S.H., "Random Arrival and the MTPT Drum Scheduling Discipline", *Proc. ACM SIGOPS Fourth Symposium on Operating System Principles,* October 1973, pp. 54–57.

*FULL75A   Fuller, S.H., Baskett, F., "An Analysis of Drum Storage Units", *Journal of the ACM,* Vol. 22, No. 1, January 1975, pp. 83–105.

*FULL75B   Fuller, S.H., "Performance Evaluation", *Introduction to Computer Architecture* (Editor: Stone, S.H.), Science Research Associates, 1975, Chapter 11.

*GRAH73A   Graham, R.M., "Performance Prediction", *Advanced Course on Software Engineering,* Springer-Verlag, 1973, pp. 395–463.

*GRAH73B   Graham, R.M., Clancy, G.J., "A Software Design and Evaluation System", *Communications of the ACM,* Vol. 16, No. 2, February 1973, pp. 110–116.

*GOTL73   Gotlieb, C.C., Metzger, J.K., "Trace Driven Analysis of a Batch Processing System", *Proc. ACM SIGSIM Symposium on the Simulation of Computer Systems,* June 1973, pp. 215–222.

*HAKO73   Hakozaki, K., Yamamoto, M., Oho, T., Ohno, N., Umemura, M., "Design and Evaluation System for Computer Architecture", *AFIPS Proc. NCC,* 1973, pp. 81–86.

*HATF72   Hatfield, D.J., "Experiments on Page Size, Program Access Patterns and Virtual Memory Performance", *IBM Journal on Research and Development,* Vol. 16, No. 1, January 1972, pp. 58–66.

*HEND74   Henderson, G., Rodriguez-Rosell, J., "The Optimal Choice of Window Sizes for Working Set Dispatching", *Proc. Second SIGMETRICS Symposium on Measurement and Evaluation,* September 1974, pp. 10–33.

*HUES67   Huesmann, L.R., Goldberg, R.P., "Evaluating Computer Systems through Simulation", *Computer Journal,* Vol. 10, No. 2, August 1967, pp. 150–156.

*HUTC73   Hutchinson, G.K., "The Use of Micro Level Simulation in the Design of a Computer Supervisory System", *Proc. ACM SIGSIM Symposium on the Simulation of Computer Systems,* June 1973, pp. 243–254.

*IHRE67   Ihrer, F.C., "Computer Performance Projected through Simulation", *Computers and Automation,* April 1967, pp. 22–27.

*KAPL73   Kaplan, K.R., Winder, R.O., "Cache Based Computer Systems", *Computer,* Vol. 6, No. 3, March 1973, pp. 30–36.

*KAY72   Kay, I.M., "An Over-the-Shoulder Look at Discrete Simulation Languages", *AFIPS Proc. SJCC,* 1972, pp. 791–798.

*KLEI70B Kleinrock, L., "Analytic and Simulation Methods in Computer Network Design", *AFIPS Proc. SJCC,* 1970, pp. 569–579.

*KNUT69 Knuth, D.E., *The Art of Computer Programming,* Volume 2: Seminumerical Algorithms, Addison-Wesley Publishing Company, 1969.

*KOBA74A Kobayashi, H., "Application of the Diffusion Approximation to Queuing Networks I: Equilibrium Queue Distributions", *Journal of the ACM,* Vol. 21, No. 2, pp. 316–328.

*KOSY73 Kosy, D.W., "An Interim Empirical Evaluation of ECSS for Computer System Simulation Development", *Proc. ACM SIGSIM Symposium on the Simulation of Computer Systems,* June 1973, pp. 79–90.

*LAVE75A Lavenberg, S.S., Slutz, D.R., "Introduction to Renerative Simulation", *IBM Journal of Research and Development,* Vol. 19, No. 5, September 1975, pp. 458–462.

*LAVE75B Lavenberg, S.S., Slutz, D.R., "Renerative Simulation of a Queuing Model of an Automated Tape Library", *IBM Journal of Research and Development,* Vol. 19, No. 5, September 1975, pp. 463–475.

MAGU72 Maguire, J.M., "Discrete Computer Simulation–Technology and Applications–The Next Ten Years", *AFIPS Proc. SJCC,* 1972, pp. 815–826.

*MATT70 Mattson, R.L., Gecsei, J., Slutz, D.R., Traiger, I.L., "Evaluation Techniques for Storage Hierarchies", *IBM Systems Journal,* Vol. 9, No. 2, 1970, pp. 78–117.

*MCDO70 MacDougall, M.H., "Computer System Simulation: An Introduction", *Computing Surveys,* Vol. 2, No. 3, September 1970, pp. 191–209.

MCDO73 MacDougall, M.H., McAlpine, S.J., "Computer System Simulation with Aspol", *Proc. ACM SIGSIM Symposium on the Simulation of Computer Systems",* June 1973, pp. 93–103.

*MURJ70 Murphey, J.O., Wade, R.M., "The IBM 360/195", *Datamation,* Vol. 16, No. 4, April 1970, pp. 72–79.

NIEL67 Nielson, N.R., "The Simulation of Time-Sharing Systems", *Communications of the ACM,* Vol. 10, No. 7, July 1967, pp. 397–412.

*NIEL69 Nielson, N.R., "ECSS: An Extendable Computer System Simulator", *Proc. Third Conference on Applications of Simulation,* December 1969, pp. 114–129.

*NOE72 Noe, J.R., Nutt, G.J., "Validation of a Trace-Driven CDC 6400 Simulation", *AFIPS Proc. SJCC,* 1972, pp. 749–757.

*NOLT73 Nolte, D.S., Talbot, M.T., "Simulation Structure for the Development of Texas Instruments' Advanced Scientific Computer",

            Proc. ACM SIGSIM Symposium on the Simulation of Computer Systems, June 1973, pp. 113–124.

*SCHA75   Schatroff, M., Tillman, C.C., "Design of Experiments in Simulator Validation", *IBM Journal on Research and Development,* Vol. 19, No. 4, May 1975, pp. 252–262.

*SEAM69   Seaman, P.H., Soucy, R.C., "Simulating Operating Systems", *IBM Systems Journal,* Vol. 8, No. 4, 1969, pp. 264–279.

*SHER72   Sherman, S., Baskett, F., Browne, J.C., "Trace-Driven Modeling and Analysis of CPU Scheduling in a Multiprogramming System", *Communications of the ACM,* Vol. 15, No. 12, December 1972, pp. 1063–1069.

*SHER73   Sherman, S.W., Browne, J.C., "Trace Driven Modeling: Review and Overview", *Proc. ACM SIGSIM Symposium on the Simulation of Computer Systems,* June 1973, pp. 201–207.

*SMIT73   Smith, A.J., "A Performance Analysis of Multiple Channel Controllers", *Proc. First Annual SICME Symposium on Measurement and Evaluation,* February 1973, pp. 37–46.

*SVOB76   Svobodova, L., Mattson, R., "The Role of Emulation in Performance Measurement and Evaluation", *Proc. International Symposium on Computer Performance Modeling, Measurement, and Evaluation,* March 1976, pp. 126–135.

TEIC66   Teichroew, D., Lubin, J.F., "Computer Simulation—Discussion of the Technique and Comparison of Languages", *Communications of the ACM,* Vol. 9, No. 10, October 1966.

*TEOR73   Teorey, J.T., Merten, A.G., "Consideration on the Level of Detail in Simulation", *Proc. ACM SIGSIM Symposium on the Simulation of Computer Systems,* June 1973, pp. 137–143.

*WILH73   Wilheim, N.C., "A General Model for the Performance of Disk Systems", *Technical Report No. 63,* Digital Systems Laboratory, Stanford University, Stanford, California, August 1973.

*WINO70   Winograd, J., Morganstein, S.J., Herman, R., "Simulation Studies of a Virtual Memory Time-Shared, Demand Paging Operating System", *Proc. of the Third SIGOPS Symposium on Operating Systems Principles,* October 1971, pp. 149–155.

Chapter 6

Measurement Tools

Of all the basic techniques, perhaps none is more
fundamental than that of measurement.

P.O. Schoderberk
Management Systems

Measurement of a computer system can be approached from two different angles. Karush calls them the stimulus approach and the analytic approach [KARU70A]. In the *stimulus approach,* the system is viewed as a "black box" that contains a limited number of known functions. The measurement consists of observing the system's response to a controlled workload. This controlled workload is provided by a benchmark in batch systems or by a special simulator in interactive systems (interactive system driver). The system response is the acceptance and the completion of individual jobs. The stimulus approach is used primarily in comparative evaluation. This includes also comparison of system performance before and after a system modification where performance is measured by external measures such as throughput and response time. The stimulus approach provides a quick test but no insight.

The *analytic approach* involves measuring the system's internal behavior. The purpose of analytic measurement is to:

1. Ensure correct operation
2. Isolate sources of current and potential problems
3. Develop understanding of the system and its environment

The category of analytic measurement is very broad. It includes hardware diagnostics, software testing, job accounting, as well as special measurements necessary for performance analysis and evaluation. For analytic measurement, special observation points must be provided in the system.

Performance evaluation projects frequently require a combination of the two approaches: analytic measurements are performed in a controlled environment provided by a reproducible workload model. Characteristics and construction of drive workload models were discussed in Chapter 4. The discussion of measurement will therefore concentrate on analytic methods.

6.1 MEASUREMENT CONCEPTS

The measurement problem is to determine:

1. What information is pertinent to a specific measurement objective,
2. Where such information can be found,
3. How it can be extracted and recorded.

The system behavior is observable through changes in the system state. The information about the system state is contained in the system's memories. In fact, the system state is the state of all system's memories (main memory, secondary memory, local storage, control latches, etc.). However, system performance analyses deal with some simplified model of the system and the system state is represented by only a small subset of the system memories. The model determines what must be measured. The more detailed is the model, the more detailed questions can be asked about the system. The model evolves on the basis of the insight developed by actual measurement.

While every hardware component has its own permanent "state" memory, the state information of a software component may be stored anywhere in the addressable memory hierarchy. However, operations of a software component can be observed as a movement of information among different levels of the memory hierarchy and supporting data and control registers (secondary memory to main memory, main memory to instruction register, main memory to accumulator, accumulator to main memory, etc.). Several examples of where state information can be extracted are given in Table 6.1.

A change in the system state marks either the beginning or the end of a period of activity (or inactivity) of a system component (a hardware component, a software component, or a process). Since several components (processes) can be active simultaneously, a change in the system state is a change in the level of system activity.

Table 6.1
Examples of State Memories for Different Measurement Problems

Measurement	Level	Components	State Memories
CPU and channel utilization	PMS	CPU channels	CPU wait/busy bit CPU supervisor/problem state bit channel busy bits channel interrupt bits
Disk storage utilization	PMS	channel disk modules	channel busy bit channel interrupt bit module busy bit module read bit module write bit module seek bit cylinder address register bits
Evaluation of system response time	OS	scheduler	memory words representing lengths of system queues and status of individual jobs in the system
Program efficiency	OS	system routines utility programs language processors	CPU wait/busy bit instruction pointer register bits
Paging efficiency	OS	memory manager virtual pages	associative registers page tables (main memory) bits: valid/invalid bits reference bits match/no match bit
Instruction opcode utilization	ISP	control unit arithmetic and logical unit	opcode register bits execute instruction control bit
Register utilization	RT	working registers control registers	register valid/invalid bit register allocated/free bit register transfer control bits

In the following discussion, "activity" is used both in connection with a single component and in place of "activity level" of the whole system. A change in the system state is called an event.[1] A software-related event is an event associated with the function of a program. Such an event occurs when the program execution reaches a certain logical point. A hardware-related event is an event generated by a hardware operation that is independent of the logical content of the currently executing program.

The system state can be described by a vector composed of binary elements representing the states (0 or 1) of individual memory elements. An activity a_k can then be represented by a logical function that has the value of 1 on a subset X_k of the set of all possible states X, $X_k \subset X$. When the activity a_k begins, the system changes from the state $x_{old} \in X_k$ (x_{old} does not belong to X_k) to the state $x_{new} \in X_k$ (x_{new} belongs to X_k). Such transition is called an initiation event e_k. When the activity a_k terminates, the system changes from the state $x_{old} \in X_k$ to the state $x_{new} \in X_k$. Such transition is called a termination event $\bar{e}_k$. Figure 6.1 is a schematic representation of concurrent activities.

Measurements can be divided into four categories according to the type of information recorded about the measured activity. Let t_0 and t be the starting time and the ending time of a measurement experiment. The measurement categories can be described as follows:

1. **Trace** An activity a_k is completely described by a sequence of pairs (t_k^i, T_k^i), where t_k^i is the time of the ith occurrence of this activity and T_k^i is the corresponding duration of this activity. This information is obtained from an event trace, which is a sequential record of all occurrences of the initiation and termination events e_k and $\bar{e}_k$ during the measurement interval $[t_0, t]$.

2. **Relative Activity** Relative activity r_k is the ratio of the total time of the activity a_k and the total elapsed time:

[1] In some literature on performance measurement of computer systems, "event" is defined as "activity." For example, the CPU being busy or the overlap of CPU and channel activities are events in this interpretation; their occurrence can be counted and their duration can be timed. In other works, an event is interpreted as the condition that must be satisfied for the system to change its state. The way it is defined here, an event is a transition from one system state to another that occurs when certain conditions are satisfied.

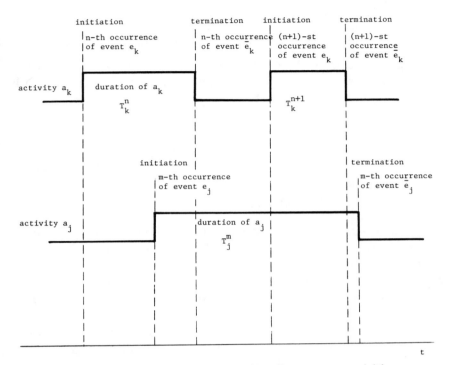

Figure 6.1. Time-chart representation of concurrent activities.

$$r_k = \frac{1}{t-t_0} \int_{t_0}^{t} a_k(\tau)\, d\tau,$$

$t \geqslant t_0$, where $a_k = 1$ if $x(\tau) \in X_k$; $a_k = 0$ otherwise.

Relative activity is frequently used as a performance measure (CPU utilization, channel utilization).

3. **Event Frequency**   The frequency of entering a particular state is measured by counting the events that represent transitions into this state. The frequency of occurrence of an activity a_k, c_k, is measured by counting the initiation events e_k:

$$c_k = \frac{1}{t-t_0} \sum_{t_n} e_k(\tau),$$

$t \geqslant t_n \geqslant t_0$, where $e_k = 1$ for $\tau = t_n$; $e_k = 0$ otherwise;

and t_n are the times of occurrence of the event e_k.

4. **Distribution of Activity Intervals**   Let $f_k^n(T)$ be the distribution of the duration times T of the activity a_k at the time of the nth termination of this activity. Then

$$f_k^n(T) = \frac{1}{n} \sum_{i=1}^{n} g(T, T_k^i),$$

where $g(T, d) = 1$ for $T = d$; $g(T, d) = 0$ otherwise.

6.2 PERFORMANCE MONITOR

A performance monitor is a tool that facilitates analytic measurements necessary for performance analysis and evaluation. The name monitor reflects the fact that performance cannot be assessed from a snapshot measurement, but only after observing (monitoring) the system for a sufficiently long time period. Monitoring usually means continuous observation of the system's behavior and utilization while the system is serving its users. Measurement, on the other hand, often means special experiments, the purpose of which is to discover performance effects of different variables. Such experiments may require that the system is driven by a reproducible workload model, thus making the system inaccessible to the user. However, the tools for collecting and processing performance data are conceptually the same, regardless of what form of workload is used to drive the system. Here, the terms monitoring and measurement are used interchangeably.

Figure 6.2 shows the basic structural elements of a performance monitor. Connection of the monitor to the measured system (sometimes referred to as the host system) is achieved through system instrumentation. The instrumentation facilitates observation of a specific set of system activities. The selector element selects a subset of observable activities for monitoring. The processing element interrogates the state of the measured system, and, based on the measurement options currently in effect, collects and prepares pertinent data to be recorded by the recording element. The interpreter element analyzes and synthesizes data accumulated by the recording element and presents the results in a meaningful form. The interpretation of

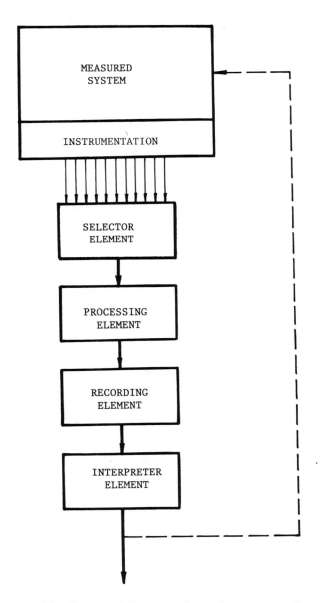

Figure 6.2. Structural elements of a performance monitor.

the accumulated data is usually a post-measurement process, but it may parallel the monitoring phase. The capability of real-time data reduction and interpretation can be utilized for dynamic control of system performance [BAUR73, BELR72].

Theoretically, activities at any system level should be measurable with the same tool. Unfortunately, heterogeneous characteristics of system memories render development of a universal measurement tool unfeasible. The rest of this chapter discusses different types of monitors, their characteristics and applicability.

6.3 SOFTWARE MONITORS

A software monitor is a special program incorporated into the software of the measured system. A software monitor is an internal tool, that is, it is supported entirely by the measured system. Such a monitor competes for system resources with jobs that constitute the system workload. The insertion of a software monitor alters the system. This phenomenon is called *monitor artifact.*

Table 6.2 describes the structural elements of a software monitor. Software instrumentation facilitates interruptions of the normal sys-

Table 6.2
Implementation of Structural Elements
of a Software Monitor

Instrumentation	Traps
	Sampling
	Interceptive
Selector element	Software switch
	Special hardware
Processing element	Software
Recording element	System's main memory
	System's secondary
	storage devices
Interpreter element	Post-process (software)
	Real-time (software)

tem processing during which the monitor can collect the necessary information. Instrumentation is frequently a combination of the listed methods. A *trap* (also called a hook, or a breakpoint) is a piece of code in the system software that transfers control to the processing element [DENI69, LONE70, BAUR73]. *Sampling instrumentation* consists of a special routine that generates timer interrupts and enables the processing element to record the system state at the instant of each such interrupt [HOLW71, KOLE71, BAUR73, SVOB73A]. *Interceptive instrumentation* utilizes the existing facilities (traps) for transferring control between levels of protection in the software hierarchy [KEEF68, LONE70].

Trap instrumentation facilitates any of the four forms of measurement: trace, relative activity, event frequency, and distribution of activity times. However, trap instrumentation presents a number of serious problems, the first in importance being modification of the system software. Insertion of monitor traps may violate the integrity of the system. Proper placement of traps requires an intimate knowledge of the system and extensive testing. Trap instrumentation can be either permanent or generated on demand. In the first case, the set of measurable events is firmly defined. Monitoring is regulated by the selector element that disables unwanted traps [DENI69]. Special hardware can greatly simplify the selection process; this topic is expanded in Chapter 7. In the second case, the monitor traps are inserted only for the time during which the system is monitored and only for those events that are monitored. Interceptive instrumentation is one example. During measurement, interlevel calls are temporarily directed to a performance monitor before passed to the appropriate level. Such temporary instrumentation is accomplished by changing the address to which the trap is made. Demand instrumentation is used mainly in program efficiency tests. A special preprocessor can insert traps into a program automatically [STUC72].

Relative duration of system activities and relative frequency of certain events can be measured by sampling techniques [KOLE71]. Instead of monitoring changes in the system state, the monitor records the state of the system at random time points, random in the sense that sampling is in no way synchronized with monitored activities. Since occurrence and duration of system activities are random variables, sampling can be performed at regular time intervals. The accuracy of the results is determined by the number of collected samples and characteristics of the sampled process. Provided that the workload is stationary, the accuracy is independent of the sampling rate. The longer the measurement interval, the lower can be the sampling rate; the monitoring overhead is lowered proportionately. Thus, in addition to the advantage of not having to modify the software of the measured system, sampling may incur less overhead than a comparable trap instrumentation. Such a situation is sketched in figure 6.3. On the other hand, sampling provides only statistical results where trap instrumentation could perhaps provide deterministic results (e.g., measuring efficiency of a program with a specific fixed input).

A software monitor can be implemented in different languages, but for efficiency reasons and because of the need to reach the hardware levels, software monitors are generally implemented in a machine language. Microprogramming facilitates implementation of very powerful internal monitors. Microinstructions provide programmed access to many hardware indicators that are normally inaccessible through the machine language implemented on the top of the microprogram level [PART76, ROBE72, SAAL72]. A microprogrammed monitor will be called a firmware monitor. "Firmware" frequently denotes read-only microprograms that implement an instruction set processor. Since microprograms can exercise control over individual bits and status indicators in a manner closer to hardware operations than to operations of conventional software, the term firmware can be used to indicate "something between hardware and software" and it is used here in this concept.

6.4 HARDWARE MONITORS

Hardware measurement tools can be either internal or external. Many present computers have built-in hardware facilities (e.g., CPU busy/wait light) that may be used as first order indicators of the system behavior [BELT72C, STAN69]. Other desirable internal hardware tools are discussed in Chapter 7.

An external hardware monitor is a free-standing device that senses electronic signals in the circuitry of the measured system and processes and records them externally to the measured system. Unless otherwise specified, the term hardware monitor is applied to such an

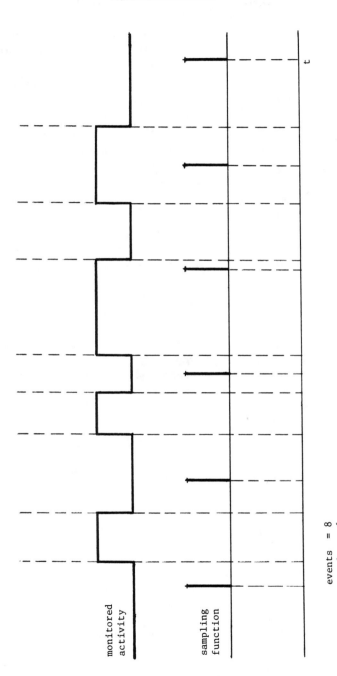

Figure 6.3. Comparison of trap instrumentation and sampling.

external device. Table 6.3 lists possible implementations of individual structural elements of a hardware monitor. A hardware monitor is a non-interfering observer; it does not require any assistance from the measured system. A simple hardware monitor consists of sensors that monitor the state of the measured system, a logic plugboard where a variety of Boolean functions can be performed on the monitored state bits (decode state and extract monitored events), a set of counters that either count event occurrences or time duration of system activities, and a display or recording unit. More advanced monitors include features such as data comparators, sequencers, random access memory, and associative memory [HUGH73A, MURP68, RUUD72]. A block diagram of a typical hardware monitor with a data comparator and a magnetic tape for recording the contents of the monitor counters is shown in figure 6.4. In addition, some hardware monitors are programmable: these include a mini-computer that provides the necessary intelligence for more elaborate measurement experiments and real-time processing of measurement

Table 6.3
Implementation of Structural Elements
of a Hardware Monitor

Instrumentation	Electronic probes (sensors)
	Plug interface
	Wired into the system
Selector element	Logical Plugboard
	Associative memory
	Software
Processing element	Logical plugboard
	Software
Recording element	Counters
	Random access memory
	Secondary storage device
Interpreter element	Software—post-process
	Software—real-time
	Hardwired display

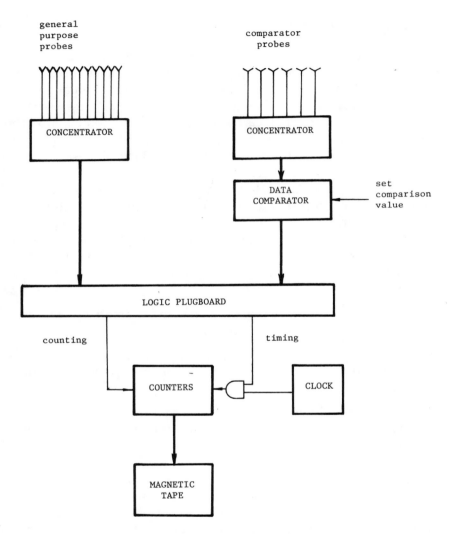

Figure 6.4. Hardware monitor.

data. A programmable monitor also facilitates online selection and switching of measurement experiments.

Several types of both non-programmable and programmable hardware monitors are produced commercially [FEDS75]. Other hardware monitors were developed at different companies as research tools for the internal use [ASCH71, HUGH73A, SHEM72].

6.5 MONITOR POWER

Measurement capabilities of both hardware and software monitors are limited by inherent physical constraints. Monitor power and monitor artifact can be used as the criteria for evaluation and selection of performance monitors. Monitor artifact, as discussed earlier, is the side effects incurred by monitor functioning. Monitor power is determined by the used technique and the actual implementation of the monitor. Monitor power has five dimensions:

1. **Monitor Domain**   Monitor domain is a class of activities theoretically observable with a particular monitoring technique.[2] Note the difference between monitor domain and instrumentation: Instrumentation facilitates application of a monitoring technique to a particular problem; it selects a unique set of measurable events that are the indicators of specific system activities from the monitor domain.

2. **Input Rate**   Input rate is the maximum frequency at which events can be recognized and recorded.

3. **Input Width**   Input width is the number of bits of input information the monitor can extract and process when a monitored event occurs.

4. **Recording Capacity**   Recording capacity is the number of memory elements that are available for storing extracted information. Recording capacity is an attribute of the recording element. It determines the amount of information that can be retained for further processing. Relative activity can be measured with an aid of a single counter. Average duration of a measured activity can be derived from two values: accumulated time of duration of all occurrences of this activity and the total number of these occurrences. Two counters are therefore sufficient. Data needed to estimate the distribution of a measured variable can be obtained from an event trace. The recording capacity necessary to hold such data may be on the order of tens or hundreds of millions of words. An alternate approach is to use the recording element as an array of counters and

---

[2] Provided that the monitor is not constrained by its physical implementation.

store the sum function $\Sigma\ g(T,\ d)$. Even though T is a set of discrete points, in general it is impossible to "remember" function values for the entire range of T. The function g thus has to be redefined to make measurement feasible:

$$g(T_j, d) = 1 \text{ if } T_j \leqslant d < T_{j+1},$$

$$g(T_j, d) = 0 \text{ otherwise,}$$

for j = 1, 2, 3, . . . , N, N being the size of the counter array.

5. **Monitor Resolution** Monitor resolution is the resolution of the time clock from which the monitor derives timing information. This factor limits the achievable accuracy of time-based measures.

6.6 LIMITATIONS OF HARDWARE AND SOFTWARE MONITORS

Neither hardware nor software monitors are usable at all levels of computer system performance measurement. In this section, these two classes of monitors are compared in terms of the dimensions defined in the preceeding section.

6.6.1 Monitor Domain

Many system activities are observable both with software and with hardware monitors. As an example, let us consider the measurement of CPU activity in the IBM S/360 or S/370. The Program Status Word (PSW) contains the CPU Wait bit, that can be directly monitored by a hardware monitor. An internal software monitor can monitor the status of the CPU by generating interrupts and interrogating the CPU Wait bit of the PSW stored by an interrupt. In this case, the state of the measured system is represented by the CPU Wait bit; the measured state is Wait=0. A different approach is to use a wait task. A wait task is a dummy task (an infinite loop using CPU only) that runs as the lowest priority job and is thus executed only if there is no real job ready for execution. The time spent in the wait task can be monitored by software means. Also, control transfers in and out of the wait task change the state of the instruction address register and the state of the control field indicating what partition is being addressed (protect key). Either the former or the latter can be chosen to represent the state of the measured system and monitored by an external hardware monitor. In general, however, the domains of hardware and software monitors significantly differ, as indicated in Figure 6.5.

Software (firmware) monitors have controlled access to those memory elements that can be read by a machine instruction (micro-instruction). A software monitor can observe hardware-related events only if they are accompanied by a control transfer to an instruction at a known (logical) address (hardware interrupts), or if they store

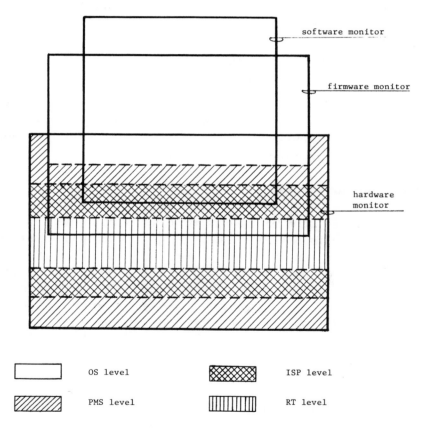

Figure 6.5. Domains of firmware, software, and hardware monitors and their overlap.

identifying information that can be later investigated by a software monitor. Peripheral devices, for example, can be monitored only on the level of their communication with the CPU. On the other hand, some descriptive information such as program names or data set names can be extracted only by an internal software monitor. Such information is necessary for identifying measured objects and tracing software operations, since many software components do not have a permanent location in the system's memory hierarchy.

Hardware monitors can monitor the state of any memory element, provided no special system generated signal is necessary to retrieve the state information. A hardware monitor cannot directly monitor the contents of a random access memory; it has access to information stored in such memory only as this information is passed through the memory port. Strictly taken, this latter is true for software monitors also. But a software monitor has the power to decide what data should be brought to it for testing or processing, whereas a hardware monitor is only a passive observer that has no control over the system's memory. A hardware monitor can sense software-related events only when accompanied by a control transfer to a fixed absolute address (hardware monitor logic decodes the contents of the instruction address register) [AMIO72], or when triggered by execution of a special instruction such as the Supervisor Call (hardware monitor logic decodes the contents of the instruction opcode register).

6.6.2 Input Rate

Hardware monitors have the ability to resolve events at high rates (usually 10 to 25 MHz). The monitoring rate of a hardware monitor is absolute: it is determined by the speed of probes and the speed of monitor logic. The domain of a software monitor does not extend beyond the programming level. The finest recognizable event is an execution of a single instruction. (For a firmware monitor, it is an execution of a single microinstruction.) The maximum input rate of a software monitor is thus derived from the maximum instruction execution rate, not counting instructions that compose the monitor. This rate is only relative: the larger the monitor overhead, the lower the input rate in absolute scale.

6.6.3 Input Width

A software monitor can detect and process events only in a sequential manner. However, a software monitor is capable of "stopping" the CPU, in the sense that it interrupts normal processing for the time necessary to gather relevant information. The input width is theoretically unlimited, the only constraint being the accompanying overhead. A hardware monitor enables detection and processing of several events occurring in parallel. The input width of hardware monitors is low, limited by the number of available probes.

6.6.4 Recording Capacity

The primary recording element of many hardware monitors consists only of a set of counters (on the order of tens). The recording capacity of hardware monitors employing a random access memory is, however, comparable to the recording capacity of software monitors. If backed up by a secondary storage device, this capacity can be made essentially unlimited.

6.6.5 Monitor Resolution

Hardware monitors measure time intervals by sampling the system's state memory at very high rate. This rate is derived from the clock built into the monitor; it can be as high as the allowable input rate. Software monitors use the timer of the measured system. Timers in older systems often have low resolution (the system timer of the S/360 has resolution of 16.7 msec). Newer systems have a high-speed hardware timer than can be read and modified with a single machine instruction (S/370 has a timer with a 1 μsec resolution).

The positive and negative characteristics of hardware and software monitors are summarized in Table 6.4. The utility of hardware monitors at the software level is only marginal; here software monitors are essential. However, a software monitor changes to some extent the character of the monitored system; the monitor artifact is a projection of such distortion. As the rate of monitored events increases, monitor demands on system resources can become significant, and the problem of monitor artifact must not be overlooked.

6.7 HYBRID MONITOR

An ideal performance monitor can be described as a monitor with unlimited power and zero artifact. The quality of an ideal monitor can be approached by a two-level instrumentation and event processing facility:

Level 1   This level consists of internal (software) instrumentation that detects software-related events; software controlled selector; software processing element that decodes events and generates appropriate signals detectable by an external hardware monitor.

Level 2   This level consists of an external hardware monitor that combines signals from Level 1 with signals corresponding to various hardware-related events and processes and records them as required.

Such monitor is called a hybrid monitor. A simplified structure of a hybrid monitor is presented in figure 6.6. The functions of a performance monitor are divided between the software of the measured system and an external device. The mechanics of passing information between the two worlds are explained next.

Conventional methods for passing information in and out of a computer system can be divided into two groups:

1. I/O devices are controlled by a special processor (I/O controller, channel) that has a direct access to the system's main memory.
2. All input and output processing is handled by the CPU that moves data between the system's memory and the I/O interface.

Both approaches can be used in performance monitoring. The first approach is highly feasible in a multiprocessor system: one of the processors can perform the monitoring function. An example is a HEMI monitor implemented on one of the peripheral processors of the CYBER system [SEBA74].

The concept of hybrid monitoring as described in the beginning of

Table 6.4

Characteristics of Software and Hardware Monitors

Software Monitors	Hardware Monitors
(N) Generally not portable, can be used only with a specific type of a CPU and operating system combination	(P) Portable, can be attached to any CPU or peripheral
(N) Measurement artifact	(P) Require no system resources
(P) Theoretically unlimited input width	(N) Input width limited to the number of available probes
(P) Powerful and flexible decoding capabilities (can handle descriptive variables)	(N) Limited decoding capabilities
(N) Events can be processed only sequentially	(P) Several events may be processed simultaneously
(P) Can access any main memory data	(N) Cannot directly monitor information stored in a random access memory
(P) Can monitor performance of software level components regardless of their location in main memory	(N) Limited measurement of software level components; possible only if actual addresses of these components remain fixed during a measurement experiment

(N) Cannot monitor events in I/O devices and switches

(N) Timer resolution often not sufficient

(N) Problem of timer synchronization with monitored events

(N) System failure terminates monitoring process

(N) Logical errors in monitor elements may cause software system failures

(P) Monitor can be easily controlled by the measured system

(N) Software instrumentation requires intimate knowledge of software operations

(P) positive factor; (N) negative factor.

(P) Several independent hardware units can be monitored simultaneously

(P) High-resolution timer

(P) Operates asynchronously to the measured system

(P) Monitoring not terminated when the monitored system fails

(N) Attachment of probes may cause hardware system failures

(N) The measured system has only limited control over the monitor

(N) Probe attachment requires skill and intimate knowledge of the RT level

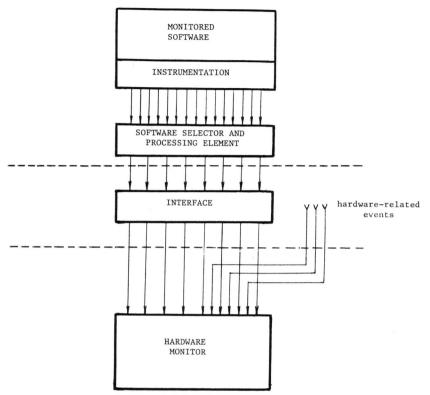

Figure 6.6. Hybrid monitor.

this section is based on the assumption that there exists a direct interface between the software of the measured system and the external world. The software instrumentation of a hybrid monitor creates a new image of the system state in memory elements that can be directly monitored by an external hardware monitor.[3] The required monitor interface, as shown in figure 6.7, is formed by a set of hardware latches, that is called here the M-register (MR). The latches can be set and reset individually or in groups, where all changes are controlled by the system software. An external monitor has direct access to any and all MR latches. Appropriate latches are set upon an occurrence of an initiation event and reset with a

---

[3] The idea of such interface occurred first in the SNUPER computer project [ESTR67B]. This project aimed for fully automated instrumentation of software that would generate signals countable by an external monitor.

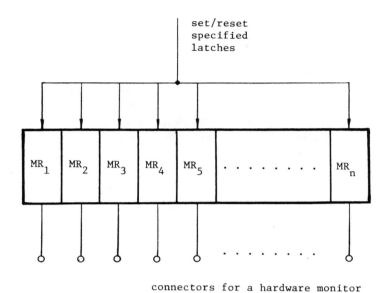

connectors for a hardware monitor

Figure 6.7. Monitor interface.

corresponding termination event; the latches remain set for the entire duration of the monitored activity. A hardware monitor can directly count occurrence and time duration of that activity. The rest of this section discusses different implementations of the monitor interface that facilitate immediate recording of events and direct timing of system activities.

6.7.1 Direct Write Interface

This type of interface requires that the image of the M-register is kept in the main memory; it is called here the virtual M-register (VMR). The software instrumentation of a hybrid monitor initiates a "Direct Write" operation causing the contents of the VMR to be transferred to the interface. Two steps, update VMR and write, are necessary to pass information to a hardware monitor. An example of this type of interface is the optional "Direct Control" feature of the IBM S/360 and S/370 [IBM71]. This feature enables the CPU to send a byte of information to and receive a byte of information from another CPU or external device. This byte of information has to be stored in main memory. While this feature was not designed for the purpose of measurement but communication, it does facilitate hybrid monitoring.

The system software can be instrumented to provide simultaneous support for several independent experiments, each experiment feeding a separate virtual M-register. This assumes that the external monitor and the interface can be multiplexed. Figure 6.8 illustrates such an arrangement. Identifiers must be passed along with the bit pattern indicating a new state to select the appropriate processing and recording element. Since the interface is multiplexed, the external monitor has to create a copy of each VMR in its own memory (EMR).

6.7.2 Memory Bus Monitor

Signals travelling the memory bus are a rich source of performance related information. These signals fall into three basic groups: memory address, data being read or written, and control information. A memory bus monitor detects events as a combination of these three types of signals. Sought combinations are determined by the contents of the address comparator register, the data comparator register, and control masks [FULL73C, FRYE73]. Figure 6.9 shows basic elements of a memory bus monitor.

The processing element supporting the software instrumentation creates a state image in the virtual M-register. The address comparator register (ACR) of a memory bus monitor is set to the VMR address. A match is set to occur when (current address = content of ACR) and (control = write), that is, a match occurs every time the VMR is changed. The Data Comparator Register (DCR) may also participate in the selection process to filter out uninteresting events. Upon a match, a new state is transferred into the Event Register (ER) that plays the role of the M-register.

Again, the system software may be instrumented to support several independent experiments. Switching of experiments is attained by changing the contents of the ACR (and DCR); this can be manual or handled by the monitor or the measured system. If the ACR is replaced by an associative memory, the memory bus monitor can also be used in a multiplexed mode, the degree of multiplexing being limited by the size of the associative memory.

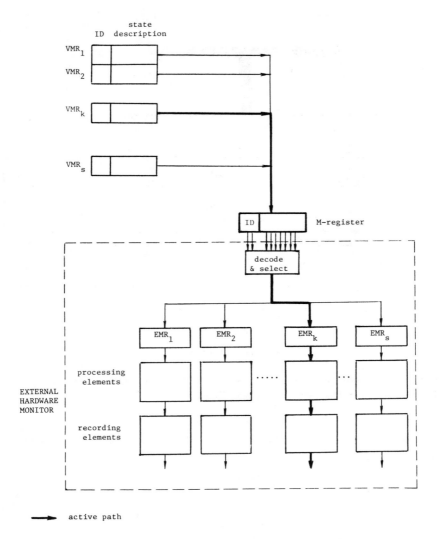

Figure 6.8. Hybrid monitoring—shared mode.

6.7.3 Directly Controllable Monitor Interface

The directly controllable monitor interface (DCMI) is a modification of the direct write interface that eliminates the necessity of duplicating the M-register in the main memory of the measured

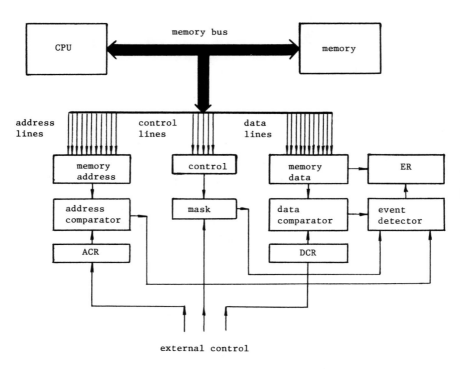

Figure 6.9. Memory bus monitor. ACR = Address Comparator Register; DCR = Data Comparator Register; ER = Event Register.

system. The DCMI consists of the M-register and the associated instructions:

Set M-register   SMR *I*

and

Clear M-register   CMR *I*

where *I* is the number (address) of the affected latch. The rest of the M-register remains unchanged.[4] Future discussions of hybrid monitoring assume that the monitor interface is implemented this way.

The monitor interface is a unique resource that can only be used

---

[4] Due to varying internal delays, simultaneously excited latches do not change their outputs at exactly the same time. The attached hardware monitor could possibly decode one or more wrong values before the M-register would reach a stable state. This problem is eliminated if only one input is allowed to change

by one process at a time, and as such, it must be under control of the system supervisor. This means that the associated instructions must be privileged; monitoring at non-privileged software levels can be accomplished only through calls to a special software component (event selector and processing element) operating in the privileged mode. A more flexible instrumentation can be achieved if a private monitor interface is provided for each level of protection. The software functions for event decoding, selection, and processing can then be merged in a single instruction, practically eliminating all software overhead.

6.8 HYBRID MONITOR DOMAIN AND APPLICATION

The main advantages of the hybrid monitor are (1) the ability to monitor software-related events with minimal artifact, and (2) a substantial reduction in a complexity of software instrumentation. Hybrid monitoring, however, is possible only if the set of distinct measured events is sufficiently small. Descriptive information (job names, data set names, input text) is generally impossible to obtain with this technique. The domain of a hybrid monitor is illustrated in figure 6.10.

The hybrid technique is particularly suitable for timing software activities. Specific examples are given in the Appendix. Additional applications include:

1. Labeling of events observable with an ordinary hardware monitor, where labels are encoded descriptive information [HUGH73B].
2. Control of an external hardware[5] monitor [SCHU67, EAST72].

---

at a time. The Direct Write interface can, of course, be programmed such that only one bit may change at a time. Otherwise, it is necessary to provide a special signal indicating when the M-register is in a stable state. This latter arrangement requires more sophistication on the side of the external hardware monitor.

[5] An external hardware monitor can be activated and deactivated under control of the system software. The TS/SPAR (Time Sharing Performance Activity Recorder) [SCHU67] was planned to be controllable by a special instruction issued by the measured system (start monitor, stop monitor). The opcode register was thus chosen to play the role of the monitor interface.

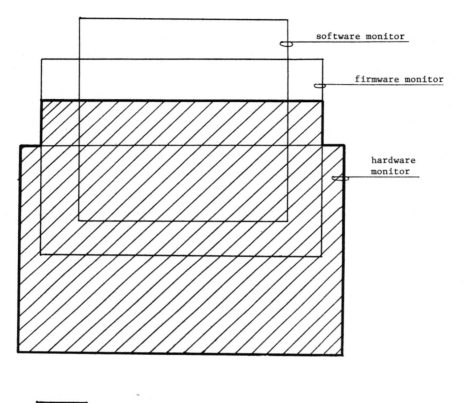

software monitor

firmware monitor

hardware
monitor

hybrid monitor

Figure 6.10. Domain of the hybrid monitor.

3. Synchronization of an external hardware monitor with an internal software monitor.

Synchronization of measurement conducted simultaneously by an external hardware monitor and an internal software monitor can take place on several different levels: the event selection level, the processing level, the recording level, or the interpretation level. The four cases are illustrated in figure 6.11.

6.9 DESIGN OF AN INTERNAL SOFTWARE MONITOR

The several preceeding sections elaborated on the concept and advantages of external monitoring and an interface through which

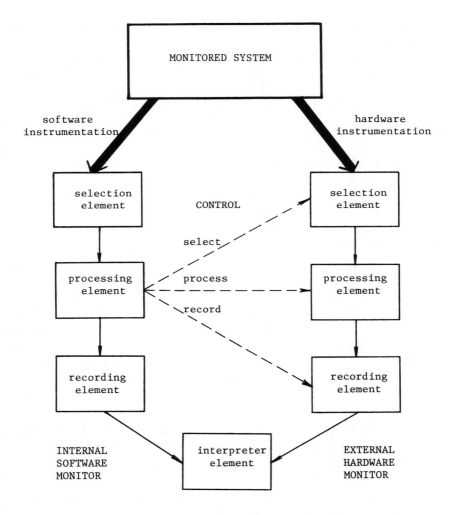

Figure 6.11. Synchronization of a hardware and a software monitor.

software related information can be passed to an external device. The hybrid technique is very efficient and effective for extracting information of a certain type. As the amount and complexity of information that must be recorded for each event increases, hybrid monitoring becomes technologically infeasible, both because of the size of the monitor interface and the complexity of the decision logic that would have to be built into the supporting external device. Thus, processing and recording of extracted information must be handled internally.

Internal software monitors are the most powerful and flexible tools, but they interfere with the monitored system by using system resources that could otherwise be used for processing users' jobs. In particular, a software monitor requires CPU time, main memory, auxiliary storage, and I/O facilities. A number of trade-offs exist; these trade-offs ought to be carefully investigated.

Some possible objectives for evaluation of the trade-offs in used resources are:

- Minimize the amount of resources used by the monitor.
- Minimize the use of the resource that is or could become a system bottleneck.

This section is concerned with a design of a software trace monitor, namely the problem of allocating the system resources to the monitor. A trace monitor creates a special record for each occurrence of each monitored event; the output of a trace monitor is a time ordered sequence of event records. From the point of resource requirements, the design of a trace monitor is basically a buffering problem that can be analyzed with a simple model. Three types of parameters are required to build the model:

1. Parameters that describe the internal structure of the monitor.
2. Parameters that describe current utilization of those resources of the measured system that are needed to support the monitor.
3. Parameters that describe the character of the monitored events.

The trace monitor performs two basic functions: it creates records that are placed into a buffer, and it transfers the content of the buffer into secondary storage. A model of this process is shown in figure 6.12. Two buffers, each capable of holding N records, are provided to ensure continuous monitoring. Let t_B be the time it takes to fill up a buffer. Let t_E be the time needed to empty a buffer, that is, the time required to transfer the buffer content to secondary storage.

The core problem of allocating system resources to a monitor is to

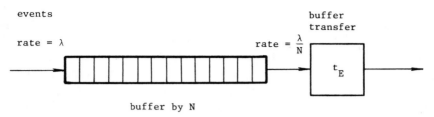

Figure 6.12. Model for analysis of resource demands of a software trace monitor.

determine how long it will take to fill up a buffer. In a real system events occur in random bursts. The level of system activity over a short time interval may be many times higher than the mean. If the buffer size is small, the time t_B is likely to fluctuate significantly. The monitor must be able to handle peak rates without unduly disturbing the measured system.

6.9.1 Design Alternatives

Several design alternatives have to be considered:

1. **Data Compression** Data collected for each event can be partially processed (compressed) prior to being entered into a record. Data compression needs additional routines that require additional CPU time and main memory. The record length also affects the size of the buffers, the required capacity of a secondary storage device, and the amount of I/O time needed to empty a buffer.

2. **Secondary Storage Device** A secondary storage device designated to serve as the monitor recording element has to be sufficiently fast and must have an adequate storage capacity. The measured system may have several different devices that could be assigned to the measurement task.

3. **Loss of Information** Loss of information may occur as a result of inconsistent instrumentation (some occurrences of monitored events are not detected), incorrect operation of the monitor routines, or insufficient capacity of the resources involved in monitoring. Only the third problem will be discussed, since monitor correctness is beyond the scope of this book.

While the content of one buffer is being transferred into secondary storage, the other buffer is being filled. If $t_E > t_B$, the buffers will overflow. An internal software monitor has the capacity of "stopping" the CPU (wait loop) until one of the buffers becomes available again. However, such action may have serious side-effects: untolerable performance degradation, in some situations perhaps even a system failure. If the monitor is not allowed to put itself to wait state, then if both buffers are full, all incoming data have to be ignored. The probability of loosing information P_L is the probability that more than N events occur in the time t_E, that is, the probability that the event rate $f > N/t_E$. In the statistical sense, loss of data may be perfectly tolerable; however, if the value of a performance measure depends on the exact sequence in which events occur in the measured system, P_L must be ensured to be extremely low.

4. **Shared Facilities**   A software monitor may impose a significant load on the supporting I/O facilities, but it also may be only moderately demanding in this respect. In the latter case, it is feasible to consider sharing of I/O facilities between the monitor and the monitored processes. The monitor interference with normal I/O activities must be kept within limits; first, it is necessary to determine the degree of utilization of potentially shared facilities. The alternatives are: (1) Dedicated channel, dedicated device; (2) Shared channel, dedicated device; or (3) Shared channel, shared device.

6.9.2 Determination of the Event Rate

The necessity of using an internal software monitor stems from the necessity to collect a large amount of descriptive information that has to be first retrieved from the system's memory. Detection of an occurrence of an event, however, requires only very little or no internal processing. The event rate can be measured with a simple hardware or hybrid monitor before the internal software trace monitor is implemented and inserted. Earlier it was said that it is not sufficient to design the buffers for the mean event rate. The event rate for a fixed time interval, the interval event rate, is a random variable with some general probability distribution. A hardware monitor can measure this distribution for $T = k \cdot \Delta t,\ k = 1, 2, \ldots,$

where Δt is the shortest possible recording interval determined by the technological characteristics of the monitor. However, it is frequently sufficient to approximate this distribution by the Poisson distribution with the parameter λ where λ is the mean event rate seen by the trace monitor. The probability of n events in time T is then

$$p_n(T) = \frac{(\lambda T)^n}{n!} e^{\lambda T}.$$

Each call to a software monitor interrupts normal processing and delays all future changes in the system state. The interevent times thus appear to be longer; the effective event rate with the software monitor inserted is lower than it would be without the monitor. Let F be the mean event rate without the monitor. If the frequency of events originating from outside of the CPU (from channels, I/O devices) is low compared to the total rate of all monitored events, then the mean interevent time changes from $1/F$ to $1/F + t_R$, where t_R is the average CPU time required to process an event and create a record. The mean effective rate is then

$$\lambda = F/(1 + F \cdot t_R).$$

6.9.3 Determination of the Constraints

As a consequence of internal software monitoring, the CPU appears to be slower by the factor $1/(1 + F \cdot t_R)$, which prolongs individual job turnaround times or response times. This degradation factor must be kept as small as possible. With respect to other resources, the main memory and the I/O facilities, the monitor behaves as an additional job. Utilization of these resources before inserting the monitor must be known in order to determine the limits to which they can be used by the monitor; such measurements can be performed with an ordinary hardware monitor. As the mean utilization of a resource approaches the maximum capacity, the result is a large performance degradation, as proved both by experience and by theoretical analysis. Thus, the fraction of resources that can be allocated to a monitor without significant side-effects is much lower than the reserve capacity of the system.

Design of a buffer supported by non-shared I/O facilities is a straightforward problem. The other two cases require many simplifying assumptions; only the worst case analyses are actually possible. Nevertheless, a model such as the one outlined here provides a useful insight for estimating the impact of a software monitor on the monitored system and evaluating possible design alternatives. The measurement needs change as the system evolves. Instead of building into a system a permanent monitor, the system should provide a facility for implementing different measurement programs that suit the current needs. This topic is further discussed in Chapter 7. Analysis of resource requirements and possible side-effects ought to be a part of such general measurement system.

BIBLIOGRAPHY

Entries marked with an asterisk (*) are referenced in the text.

*AMIO72   Amiot, L.W., Aschenbrenner, R.A., Natarajan, M.K., "Evaluating a Remote Batch Processing System", *Computer,* September/October 1972, pp. 24–29.

*ASCH71   Aschenbrenner, R.A., Amiot, L.W., Natarajan, M.K., "The Neurotron Monitor System", *AFIPS Proc. FJCC,* 1971, pp. 31–37.

*BAUR73   Bauer, M.J., McCredie, J.W., "AMS: A Software Monitor for Performance Evaluation and System Control", *Proc. First Annual SICME Symposium on Measurement and Evaluation,* February 1973, pp. 147–160.

BELT71   Bell, T.E., "Computer Performance Analysis: Measurement Objectives and Tools", RAND Report R-584-NASA/PR, February 1971.

*BELT72C   Bell, T.E., "Choose Your Tools to Check Your Computer", *Computer Decisions,* Vol. 4, No. 11, November 1972, pp. 12–15.

BELT72E   Bell, T.E., "Computer Performance Analysis: Minicomputer-Based Hardware Monitoring", RAND Report R-696-PR, June 1972.

BONN69   Bonner, A.T., "Using System Monitor Output to Improve Performance", *IBM Systems Journal,* Vol. 8, No. 4, 1969, pp. 290–298.

BORD71   Bordsen, D.T., "Univac 1108 Hardware Instrumentation System", *Proc. ACM SIGOPS Workshop on System Performance Evaluation,* April 1971, pp. 1–28.

CARL71   Carlson, G., "A User's View of Hardware Performance Monitors or How to Get More Computer for Your Dollar", *Proc. of IFIP Congress 1971,* v. 2, pt. 5, pp. 128–132.

CURE72   Cureton, H.O., "A Philosophy to System Measurement", *AFIPS Proc. FJCC,* 1972, pp. 965–969.

*DENI69   Deniston, W.R., "SIPE: A TSS/360 Software Measurement Technique", *Proc. 24th ACM National Conference,* 1969, pp. 229–245.

DRUM73   Drummond, M.E., *Evaluation and Measurement Techniques for Digital Computer Systems,* Prentice-Hall, 1973.

*EAST72   East, D.G., Davis, C.C., Phillips, R.D., "Relocate and Multi-processor Map and Trace Monitor", *IBM Technical Disclosure,* September 1972, pp. 1377–1378.

*ESTR67B   Estrin, G., Hopkins, D., Coggan, B., Crocker, S.D., "SNUPER Computer–A Computer in Instrumentation Automation", *AFIPS Proc. SJCC,* Thompson Books, Washington, D.C., 1967, pp. 645–656.

*FEDS75   FEDSIM Report, "Hardware Monitor Specifications Comparison: Tesdata Systems Corp. and COMPRESS, Division of COMTEN, Inc., R-75-1, January 1975.

FERR72B   Ferrari, D., "Firmware-Monitoring Tools for Measuring the Performance of Microprogrammed Computer Systems", *Proc. of 2nd ACM International Computing Symposium,* Venice, 1972, pp. 83–90.

FOLE74   Foley, J.D., McInroy, J.W., "An Event-Driven Data Collection and Analysis Facility for a Two-Computer Network", *Proc. Second Annual SIGMETRICS Symposium on Measurement and Evaluation,* September 1974, pp. 106–120.

*FRYE73   Fryer, R.E., "The Memory Bus Monitor–A New Device for Developing Real-Time Systems", *AFIPS Proc. NCC,* 1973, pp. 75–79.

*FULL73C   Fuller, S.H., Swan, R.J., Wulf, W.A., "The Instrumentation of C.mmp, A Multi-Mini-Processor", *Proc. COMPCON 73 (Digest of Papers),* Seventh Annual IEEE Comp. Soc. International Conference, 1973, pp. 173–176.

GROC69   Grochow, J.M., "Real Time Graphic Display of Time-Sharing System Operating Characteristics", *AFIPS Proc. FJCC,* 1969, pp. 379–386.

*HOLW71   Holtwick, G.M., "Designing a Commercial Performance Measurement System", *Proc. ACM SIGOPS Workshop on System Performance Evaluation,* April 1971, pp. 29–58.

*HUGH73A   Hughes, J., Cronshaw, D., "On Using a Hardware Monitor as an Intelligent Peripheral", *ACM SICME Performance Evaluation Review,* No. 4, December 1973, pp. 3–19.

*HUGH73B   Hughes, J., "Case Histories–Using a Hardware Monitor as an Intelligent Peripheral", *ACM SICME Performance Evaluation Review, Interface of Computer Science and Statistics,* October 1973.

*IBM71   "IBM System/360 and System/370 Direct Control and External

Interruption Features", *IBM Systems Reference Library,* GA22-6845-3, July 1971.

*KARU70A   Karush, A.D., "Two Approaches for Measuring the Performance of Time-Sharing Systems", *Software Age,* March 1970, pp. 10–13.

KARU70B   Karush, A.D., "Two Approaches for Measuring the Performance of Time-Sharing Systems (Conclusion)", *Software Age,* May 1970, pp. 13–14.

*KEEF68   Keefe, D.D., "Hierarchical Control Programs for Systems Evaluations", *IBM Systems Journal,* Vol. 7, No. 2, 1968, pp. 123–133.

KOLE71   Kolence, K.W., "A Software View of Measurement Tools", *Datamation,* Vol. 17, No. 1, January 1, 1971, pp. 32–38.

*LONE70   Lonergan, R., Androsciani, V., "SUPERMON, A Software Monitor for Performance Evaluation", *Technical Memo No. 30,* Stanford Computation Center, Stanford, California, January 1970.

MURP68   Murphy, R.W., "The System Logic and Usage Recorder", *AFIPS Proc. FJCC,* 1969, pp. 219–229.

NEME71   Nemeth, A.G., Rovner, P.D., "User Program Measurement in a Time-Shared Environment", *Communications of the ACM,* Vol. 14, No. 10, October 1971, pp. 661–666.

NOE74   Noe, J.D., "Acquiring and Using a Hardware Monitor", *Datamation,* April 1974, pp. 89–95.

NUTT75   Nutt, G.J., "Tutorial: Computer System Monitors", *Computer,* Vol. 8, No. 11, November 1975, pp. 51–61.

*PART76   Partridge, D.R., Card, R.E., "Hardware Monitoring of Real-Time Aerospace Computer Systems," *Proc. International Symposium on Computer Performance Modeling, Measurement and Evaluation,* March 1976, pp. 85–101.

PETE74   Peterson, T.G., "A Comparison of Software and Hardware Monitors", *ACM Performance Evaluation Review,* Vol. 3, No. 3, September 1973, pp. 2–5.

PINK69   Pinkerton, T.B., "Performance Monitoring in a Time-Sharing System", *Communications of the ACM,* Vol. 12, No. 11, November 1969, pp. 608–610.

RODR72   Rodriguez-Rosell, J., Dupuy, J., "The Evaluation of a Time-Sharing Page Demand System", *APIPS Proc. SJCC,* 1972, pp. 759–765.

*ROBE72   Roberts, L.W., "Performance Measurement with Microcode", presented at the *Seminar on Computer System Performance Measurements,* Whippany, New Jersey, June 14–15, 1972.

ROEK69   Roek, D.J., Emerson, W.C., "A Hardware Instrumentation Approach to Evaluation of a Large Scale System", *Proc. 24th ACM National Conference,* 1969, pp. 351–367.

*RUUD72   Ruud, R.J., "The CPM-X—A System Approach to Performance Measurement", *AFIPS Proc. FJCC,* 1972, pp. 949—951.

*SAAL72   Saal, H.J., Shustek, L.J., "Microprogrammed Implementation of Computer Measurement Techniques", *Proc. ACM 5th Annual Workshop on Microprogramming,* September 1972, pp. 42—50.

SALT70   Saltzer, J.H., Gintell, J.W., "The Instrumentation of Multics", *Communications of the ACM,* Vol. 13, No. 8, August 1970, pp. 495—500.

*SCHU67   Schulman, F.D., "Hardware Measurement Device for IBM System/360 Time Sharing Evaluation", *Proc. 22nd ACM National Conference,* 1967, pp. 103—114.

SCHW73   Schwartz, J.M., Wyner, D.S., "Use of the SPASM Software Monitor to Evaluate the Performance of the Burroughs B6700", *AFIPS Proc. NCC,* 1973, pp. 93—100.

*SEBA74   Sebastian, P.R., "Hybrid Events Monitoring Instrument", *Proc. Second Annual SIGMETRICS Symposium on Measurement and Evaluation,* September 1974, pp. 127—139.

SEDG70   Sedgewick, R., Stone, R., McDonald, J.N., "SPY—A Program to Monitor OS/360", *AFIPS Proc. FJCC,* 1970, pp. 119—128.

*SHEM72   Shemer, J.E., Robertson, J.B., "Instrumentation of Time-Shared Systems", *Computer,* Vol. 5, No. 4, July/August 1972, pp. 39—48.

*STAN69   Stanley, W.I., "Measurement of System Operational Statistics", *IBM Systems Journal,* Vol. 8, No. 4, 1969, pp. 299—308.

*STUC72   Stucki, L.G., "A Prototype Automatic Program Testing Tool", *AFIPS Proc. FJCC,* 1972, pp. 829—836.

SVOB73A   Svobodova, L., "Online System Performance Measurements with Software and Hybrid Monitors", *Proc. ACM SIGOPS Fourth Symposium on Operating System Principles,* October 1973, pp. 45—53.

WARN70   Warner, D., "Hardware Techniques", *SIGCOSIM Newsletter,* No. 8, Part II, August 1970, pp. 9—18.

Chapter 7

Measurability of Computer Systems

The complexity of current computer systems makes measurement necessary, and also difficult. This difficulty is accentuated by the fact that the hardware and the software of conventional computer systems is generally not designed to be monitored. As a result, some types of measurements require unnecessarily complicated tools, and can be very expensive in terms of the system's resources consumed during the measurements. Most seriously, some types of measurements may not even be possible without substantially altering the system.

Chapter 6 described the functions of a performance monitor and discussed the advantages and limitations of different monitoring techniques. However, it is the hardware and the software of each individual system that determines what can be measured and how it can be measured. The commitment to protect users' privacy is an additional constraint. This chapter looks at the measurement problem from a different angle: it examines the measurability of computer systems.

Measurability of a computer system can be defined in terms of the total set of information accessible to performance monitors and the cost of measurement. However, it is necessary to discriminate between what is not allowed to be measured because of privacy requirements and what cannot be measured or is costly to measure because of technological obstacles (e.g., physical reachability of test points, properties of the internal timing mechanism). The measurability spectrum ranges from complete measurability where it is possible to monitor every single system component and function and all interactions between the system components to cases where the only way to measure a system is by observing its external response (e.g., requested task completed) to an external stimulus (execute user command). Even such external measurement, however, may be prohibited for security reasons.

Measurement needs vary with the complexity, the designation, and the stage of development of a computer system. Measurements can be divided into two categories:

1. Measurements requested (and analyzed and evaluated) by a user.
2. Measurements required by the system itself.

Included in the first category are measurements of resource utilization of a production system required for configuration optimization and system growth planning as well as very detailed measurements of a system under development. In the second category are measurements that control system performance in a dynamically changing environment.

Measurement needs must be anticipated in the early states of a computer system design, such that the final product is physically measurable under changeable privacy requirements. System measurability can be achieved only with an integrated hardware-software approach. The required measurement system is a hierarchy of hardware and software components:

1. Internal hardware components that automatically detect monitored events and record data without disturbing the system.
2. Software and hardware mechanisms that assist in implementation, verification, attachment and detachment, and activation and deactivation of internal measurement routines.
3. An external monitoring device that complements the internal monitor.
4. Software and hardware protection mechanism that prevents uncontrolled monitoring of system and users' processes and data.

7.1 MEASURABILITY AND PRIVACY

When discussing the measurability problems, it is necessary to distinguish between the problems of measuring the virtual system of a single user and measuring the real system serving multiple users. Each user should be able to measure not only his own programs, but also the use of the resources that compose his virtual system. The system manager must be able to monitor all system software, as well as the usage of all hardware resources. A question arises whether and to what extent the system manager should be allowed to monitor how individual users use individual system components. If he knows what the users are trying to do, it may help him to improve system performance. On the other hand, such observations may threaten the privacy of the system users.

In general, it is necessary to define the access domain of a monitor and prevent the monitor from gathering any information outside this domain. For example, suppose that the system manager wishes to optimize the distribution of the existing data bases across the physical storage devices. For that, it is necessary to know the demand pattern for individual objects in the data bases. The system manager can obtain this information by measuring the usage of the storage assigned to individual objects; he should not be allowed to examine the purpose and the information content of objects in a private data base. This policy must be enforced by the system. Finally, it must be possible to protect the monitor itself, since it has the power to collect private data about the system under its jurisdiction.

The access rights and protection of an internal software monitor can be controlled by the same protection mechanism that controls all other processes in a system.[1] Pure hardware monitoring, however, represents an uncontrollable threat to privacy. Saltzer expressed his concern about the opportunities that various lights and switches of the operator's console offer to those initiated [SALT74]. Hardware monitors can be misused in a similar way. Hardware monitors can be connected directly to a memory port, bus, or an I/O channel, thus having easy access to all information flowing between the levels of the system information storage hierarchy. The risk of uncontrolled penetration by an external hardware monitor can be avoided if no externally accessible points are provided in the system hardware. However, such points are needed for diagnostic measurement. The second solution is to have the selector and the processing element of an external monitor under a strict control of the measured system.

The question that remains to be answered is how much of that which cannot be measured because of privacy restrictions is truly needed for a successful system improvement and planning of new systems. This question must be answered for each system individually, but in general, privacy requirements conflict with the need

---

[1] The PRIME system developed at the University of California in Berkeley represents a unique solution. The objective of high privacy led to a distributed hardware and software architecture, which in turn influenced the design of system measurement tools: the measurement tools are physically distributed with strictly defined jurisdiction [FERR73].

to find out what the users want from the system, thus making development of a representative test workload an open problem.

7.2 MEASUREMENT ENVIRONMENT

As discussed in the preceeding chapter, internal software instrumentation has distinct advantages, but such instrumentation requires an intimate knowledge of system operations and freedom to modify the system software. It is best implemented during early stages of the system software design [CAMB68, DENI69, SALT70]. However, the total set of variables that one may want to measure during the system lifetime is most likely not known at these early design stages. As a system develops, the measurement needs develop too, and the monitoring functions must be expanded. Even in a production-oriented installation, general dissatisfaction with a system that does not match the application needs may generate needs for more thorough measurements than initially anticipated.

Instead of giving a user an inflexible monitoring package, the system ought to provide a basic environment that enables a user to build a monitor satisfying his own specifications. This philosophy guided the development of the Informer measurement tool for the SDS-940 at the University of California in Berkeley [DEUT71], succeeded by the SMT (Software Measurement Tool) for the PRIME system [FERR74]. In addition to using standard measurement routines that are already a part of the SMT, users can add their own routines that best suit their purpose. User measurement routines may be inserted dynamically and called from selected points in the measured system A similar philosophy is used in the DAME (Dynamic Analysis and Modeling Environment) system that addresses the problem of program execution analysis, including performance analysis [AYGU73].

An example of a lower level system provided support for measurements is the monitor call in the IBM S/370 [KATZ71]. The "Monitor Call" (MC) instruction operates similarly to "Supervisor Call" (SVC) instruction. A special control register functions as a mask for different monitoring classes. A special privileged instruction can change the mask. This hardware provides an effective mechanism for selecting measurements that are to be in effect during different time intervals.

7.3 DATA ACQUISITION

The measurability problems are not solved by adding a mechanism that facilitates flexible insertion and deletion of measurement routines. It is the process of extracting data, the process carried out by individual measurement routines, that needs a special system support. This problem gains more weight when measurement is a part of a control process. Many components of an operating system have to have their own monitor and control functions that help the system to adapt to a dynamically changing workload. For example, the memory allocation mechanism in paging systems collects data about page usage; this information drives the page replacement algorithm. A processor scheduler can measure the amount of service already received by a job and use this information to determine the job's priority in the view of the current total load. Control decisions must be based on the performance of a system in the immediate past. A moving window estimator [DENN68] or an exponential estimator [MILL71, SALT70] is needed to assert the immediate performance.[2] The associated measurement overhead can be reduced by simple hardware.

Much performance data can be extracted without any special difficulties; other measurements are unnecessarily awkward. This applies primarily to measuring duration of system activities, as discussed earlier. Such measurements are best performed by hardware. The measured activity must be represented by an electronic signal that is then sampled by a high frequency clock without inducing any overhead. Moreover, overlap of different activities is easily detected from a logical combination of corresponding signals. This is where hardware monitors are superior to software monitors.

Much of what can be done by an external hardware monitor could be done by hardware internal to the measured system. In addition, data gathered with the aid of special internal hardware elements can easily be made available to software measurement routines upon request.

---

[2] The properties and applications of these estimators are discussed in [DENN71].

7.4 HARDWARE AIDS FOR INTERNAL MONITORING

This section discusses the structure and the utility of various internal hardware monitoring aids. The hardware components assisting in the internal measurement process must be:

Program Readable   That is, it must be possible to test the state of the component with an instruction available to the programmer.

Program Controllable   That is, it must be possible to change the state of the component with an instruction available to the programmer.

7.4.1 Timing Meters

A timing meter measures time duration of an activity by sampling the state of a memory element (or elements) associated with that activity. As figure 7.1 indicates, a timing meter is a binary counter driven by a clock derived either from the basic CPU clock or from a special generator. A 32-bit binary counter can measure and accumulate time intervals up to approximately 1.2 hours with 1 microsecond resolution (1 MHz clock), or 1200 hours with 1 millisecond resolution (1 kHz clock).

System Timer.   A hardware system timer is a standard feature of many present computers. Application:

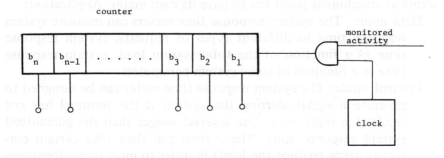

Figure 7.1.   Timing meter.

Data mode: The system timer provides time stamps for monitored events (time-of-day clock).

Control mode: The system timer generates interrupts that can be used to drive sampling monitors (interval timer).

CPU Meter   The CPU meter measures utilization of the CPU (the amount of time the CPU is busy).

Channel Meter   The channel meter measures utilization of the I/O channel (the amount of time the I/O channel is busy).

Virtual Clock   The virtual clock is a meter that measures the CPU time used by a user's job. The virtual clock is started when the job is allocated the CPU. The virtual clock is advanced only if instructions are executed on behalf of the user's job. The clock is not advanced while the CPU is handling interrupts and page faults. While each job in the system must have its own virtual clock, the actual implementation requires only one hardware meter per processor. The value of this meter must be saved as a part of the job's state. When a job is assigned a processor the virtual clock meter in this processor is reset to the value of the job's virtual clock.

Program Timer   The program timer measures time spent in executing a specific section of code. The program timer has two address bound registers loaded with relative (virtual) addresses of the beginning and the end of the measured section. The timer is advanced only when instructions are executed from that particular section, i.e., time needed to execute outer subroutines and possible interrupts is not included.

System Response Time Meters   These meters measure the system response time to requests initiated from the user terminals. Each terminal attachment point has to have its own meter. Application:

Data mode: The system response time meters can measure system response time to different types of requests, system response time as a function of the total system load, system response time as a function of some system parameters.

Control mode: The system response time meter can be designed to generate a signal alerting the system if the terminal has not received a reply in a time interval longer than the guaranteed system response time. The system can then take certain corrective steps (reduce the load) in order to meet its performance obligations.

General Purpose Timer   The general purpose timer can measure duration of any software controlled activity. This is accomplished by turning the timer on and off by instructions injected into the system software.

7.4.2 Counting Meters

Compared to methods for timing activity duration, counting of event occurrences is simple and straightforward. Special hardware counters are nevertheless justified, since some events occur with such high frequency that overhead induced by programmed counting would be intolerable. Moreover, some interesting events are normally not observable at the programming level. A counting meter is shown in figure 7.2.

Memory Reference Meter   The memory reference meter counts all references to a particular section of the main memory. The addresses of the first and the last word of the measured section are loaded into the associated address bound registers. Application:

Data mode: The memory reference meter facilitates measurement of parameters such as memory reference rate, memory utilization, memory references between page faults.

Control mode: The memory reference meter can be instrumented to generate regular interrupts (every n references) for the purpose of examining the locality of reference.

Interference Meter   The interference meter measures congestion of a system component such as a memory block or a channel. It counts requests for this component that cannot be satisfied immedi-

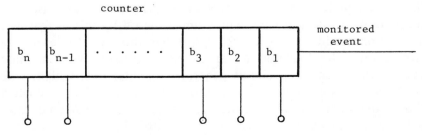

Figure 7.2. Counting meter.

ately. As the number of processors in a multiprocessor system increases, the degree of interference becomes a significant performance factor.

7.4.3 Traps

A trap is a mechanism that automatically detects an occurrence of an event and calls the monitor processing element to examine and record the event.

Jump Trap   A jump trace is a useful debugging tool as well as a performance measurement tool. It provides information about the flow of control in a program, and, if each jump instance is time-stamped, can be used to measure time spent in different program sections. The concept is simple, the mechanics are not. In conventional systems, jump trace can be acquired either by an external hardware monitor that may not be able to obtain all the information required [BORD71] or by an interpretive program that examines every single instruction in search for jump instructions. A much simpler solution is to build a trap mechanism directly into each jump instruction, such that an execution of a jump, unless masked off, will automatically cause a trap to either a standard system routine or a user-supplied routine. In microprogrammed processors, even the recording of a jump can be made a part of the instruction itself [SVOB76].

General Purpose Event Trap   An IBM S/360 and S/370 hardware debugging aid, the address match circuit [IBM70] is an example of a general purpose event trap mechanism. The memory address to be matched is loaded into the address match register manually through toggle switches. When a reference is made to this address, the address match circuit generates a pulse. However, this pulse is not recognized by the software, which limits the utility of this feature as a monitoring aid. As an aid for a software monitor, the event trap circuit must be loadable under program control. When a match occurs, this event trap circuit generates an interrupt, which, when honored, transfers control to a monitor routine. This mechanism thus provides a remote trap, i.e., it enables system instrumentation without any physical changes to the monitored programs. The event trap mechanism can be augmented to allow simultaneous monitoring of two or more events: instead of having a single address match register, the comparison is made against an associative memory that holds descriptions of several different events. Remote instrumentation can be temporary, such as for testing monitor routines, or permanent if for some reason the monitored software cannot be modified.

7.5 INTERNAL AIDS FOR EXTERNAL MEASUREMENT DEVICES

If the special hardware monitoring facilities discussed in the previous section are included in the system, is there still any need for external monitors? The answer is yes. This need occurs on two different levels:

(1) **Measurement of Activities not Measurable with an Internal Monitor**   It is impossible to build an internal meter for every single operation that a user may desire to measure at some point of time. An external hardware monitor is a flexible general purpose tool capable of monitoring any operation represented in a form of an electronic signal. Thus, an external monitor can be used to *complement* the internal monitor where internal support is not provided.

(2) **Reduction of Monitoring Artifact**   The special monitoring facilities described in the preceeding section aid in extracting hardware related data, but often a significant amount of real-time processing is still necessary. Part of this processing, such as decoding, logical operations on monitored activities, and recording, can be relegated to an external device. A programmable external monitor facilitates online analysis of measurement data, which in turn can be used for dynamic control of system performance. In both cases, an external hardware monitor is used as an *extension* of an internal monitor, such that flexibility and effectiveness of internal monitoring is combined with efficiency of external monitoring.

One possible combination of internal and external facilities was presented in Chapter 6. Since the DCMI interface is fully controlled by the software of the measured system the information passed to the monitor can undergo the same protection checks as any other object in the system.

Measurement Panel   Attachment of monitor sensors to pins provided in the system circuitry is generally a delicate task. It is advisable to manipulate the sensors only during maintenance or test periods. It is sometimes difficult to reach selected measurement points and this is likely to get worse with further development and use of the LSI technology. Errors can result from accidentally attaching a sensor to a wrong point; such errors may be difficult to detect. Also, it may be necessary to disconnect the sensors temporarily during system maintenance. However, the most serious and annoying problem is that monitor probes do impose a definite load on the measured system that may cause a system failure. All these factors become especially significant when operating a hardware monitor close to its maximum speed [NOE74]. An answer to these problems is a special measurement panel that

1. Concentrates the externally monitored entities in an easily accessible location;
2. Is sufficiently robust to withstand the load caused by a monitor and to allow changes in instrumentation while the system is operating in its normal mode [HUGH73C].

7.6 AUTOMATIC CONTROL OF SYSTEM PERFORMANCE

A desirable property of a computer system is the capability of maintaining a specified level of performance. This implies that:

1. Performance is constantly monitored;
2. It is possible to influence it by changing one or more internal or external parameters;
3. It is known how these parameters must be changed in order to bring performance to the specified level.

Performance must be represented by a measurable variable that becomes the controlled variable. The difference between the current level of the controlled variable and the prescribed level drives the control mechanism.

A computer system has many built-in controls without which the system could not function, and many controls that influence system performance, but only in a few existing computer systems control is exercised on the basis of currently observed system performance.

Figure 7.3 illustrates the mechanism of performance control in a computer system. Each job from the system input stream is represented by a sequence of service demands. The service demands are translated by the system into resource demands. The mapping from the job's service demands to the resource demands is influenced by many factors: software that supervises and performs the requested services, supporting hardware, system configuration. Additional resource demands occur as a result of multiplexing hardware resources (for example, processor time needed to handle page faults). The resource demands are satisfied in an order dictated by scheduling policies and priorities assigned either externally or internally by the system itself. The performance control changes the two-stage mapping from a set of pending service demands into the set of the actual system resources with the goal of bringing the system performance to a prescribed level.

In general, the performance objective is to maximize system throughput while providing a satisfactory response time (turnaround time). This objective can be achieved by resource management policies as long as the current total load does not exceed a level for which the required response time can be provided. Below this level, throughput can be increased by load balancing. Above this level, response time can be kept within limits only through load leveling, that is, some users must be denied service in order to provide good service to users already using the system [BAUR73, WILK71].

To be able to guarantee a specific level of performance under varying load, scheduling decisions must be coordinated and based on the current level of performance. The OS/VS2 Release 2 with the System Resource Manager (SRM) is an example of a working system of this type [LYNC74]. The controlled performance measure is the service rate received by individual jobs. The SRM aims to maximize the system throughput while at the same time providing a service rate specified by a load-dependent service curve.

Given the same set of service demands from a single user, this set does not always have to be translated into the same set of resource demands. As in resource scheduling, the system can use knowledge of its current performance to direct this translation. For example, the

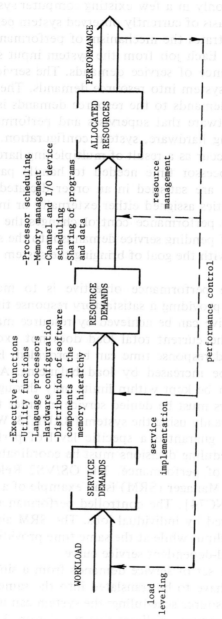

Figure 7.3. Performance control in a computer system.

system may apply a translation policy that generates lighter demands on system memory for the price of more CPU time.

Automatic control of computer system performance is a nontrivial problem. First, it combines the problems involved in performance monitoring, analysis, and evaluation. In addition, it is necessary to solve the problem of the feedback. There can be a substantial time delay between the cause and the detection of the change in the system behavior. There can also be a substantial time delay between the accepting of a decision and the enforcement of that decision. An improperly adjusted control may introduce instability into the system [WILK71]. More research is necessary to determine what parameters can be controlled and how effective such automatic control can be.

7.7 CONCLUDING REMARKS

The present complexity of performance measurement, performance analysis, and performance evaluation is a result of a great complexity of multiprogrammed and time-shared systems. Future computer systems may consist of a network of non-shared independent miniprocessors with on-demand access to a common data base, and some measures, important today, will become virtually irrelevant (e.g., utilization of local hardware resources). But while complexity and urgency of measurement problems may shift, the need to measure will not disappear. Special hardware and special software functions can considerably simplify the task of performance measurement in a multi-user system as well as a single-user system. Measurement, and consequently analysis and control of system performance, are easier if a system is designed to be measurable.

BIBLIOGRAPHY

Entries marked with an asterisk (*) are referenced in the text.

*AYGU73   Aygun, B.O., "Environments for Monitoring and Dynamic Analysis of Execution", *Proc. ACM SIGSIM Symposium on the Simulation of Computer Systems,* June 1973, pp. 179–197.

*BURK73   Burke, E.L., "A Computer Architecture for System Performance Monitoring", *Proc. First Annual SICME Symposium on Measurement and Evaluation,* February 1973, pp. 161–169.

*CAMP68   Campbell, D.J., Heffner, W.J., "Measurement and Analysis of Large Operating Systems During System Development", *AFIPS Proc. FJCC,* 1968, pp. 903–914.

*DENI69   Deniston, W.R., "SIPE: A TSS/360 Software Measurement Technique", *Proc. of 24th ACM National Conference,* 1969, pp. 229–245.

*DENN68   Denning, P.J., "The Working Set Model for Program Behavior", *Comm. ACM,* Vol. 11, No. 5, May 1968, pp. 323–333.

*DENN71   Denning, P.J., Eisentein, B.A., "Statistical Methods in Performance Evaluation", Proc. ACM SIGOPS Workshop on System Performance Evaluation, April 1971, pp. 284–307.

*DEUT71   Deutsch, P., Grant, C.A., "A Flexible Measurement Tool for Software Systems", Proc. of IFIP Congress 1971, v. 2, pt. 3, pp. 7–12.

ESTR74   Estrin, G., "Measurable Computer Systems", *Infotech State of the Art Report 18,* 1974, pp. 283–299.

FERR72A   Ferrari, D., "Workload Characterization and Selection in Computer Performance Measurement", *Computer,* Vol. 5, No. 4, July/August 1972, pp. 18–24.

*FERR73   Ferrari, D., "Architecture and Instrumentation in a Modular Interactive System", *Computer,* Vol. 6, No. 11, November 1973, pp. 25–29.

*FERR74   Ferrari, D., Liu, M., "A General-Purpose Software Measurement Tool", *Proc. Second SIGMETRICS Symposium on Measurement and Evaluation,* September 1974, pp. 94–103.

*FULL73   Fuller, S.H., Swan, R.J., Wulf, W.A., "The Instrumentation of C.mmp, a Multi-Mini-Processor", *Digest of Papers, IEEE COMPCON 1973,* pp. 173–176.

*HUGH73C   Hughes, J., "Performance Evaluation Techniques and System Reliability—A Practical Approach", ACM/NBS Performance Evaluation Workshop, March 1973.

*KATZ71   Katzan, H., *Computer Organization and the System/370,* Van Nostrand/Reinhold Company, 1971.

*LYNC74   Lynch, H.W., Page, J.B., "The OS/VS2 Release 2 System Resources Manager", *IBM Systems Journal,* Vol. 6, No. 4, 1974, pp. 274–291.

*MILL71   Mills, R.G., "The CTSS Load Leveller", *Proc. ACM SIGOPS Workshop on System Performance Evaluation,* April 1971, pp. 319–320.

*NOE74   Noe, J.D., "Acquiring and Using a Hardware Monitor", *Datamation,* April 1974, pp. 89–95.

*SALT70   Saltzer, J.H., Gintell, J.W., "The Instrumentation of Multics", *Comm. of ACM,* Vol. 13, No. 8, August 1970, pp. 495–500.

*SALT74   Saltzer, J.H., "Protection and Control of Information Sharing in Multics", *Comm. of ACM,* Vol. 17, No. 7, July 1974, pp. 388–402.

*SVOB76   Svobodova, L., Mattson, R., "The Role of Emulation in Performance Measurement and Evaluation", *Proc. International Symposium on Computer Performance Modeling, Measurement and Evaluation,* March 1976, pp. 126–135.

*WILK71   Wilkes, M.V., "Automatics Load Adjustment in Time-Sharing Systems", *Proc. of ACM SIGOPS Workshop on System Performance Evaluation,* April 1971, pp. 308–320.

Appendix

Instrumentation and Measurement of System *S*

This Appendix discusses specific measurement problems and their solutions. A case study of hybrid monitoring of a hypothetical system *S* is presented. The system *S* is a reasonably complex system with features that can be found in many present computer systems. The system *S* is instrumented for measurement of the CPU utilization profile, measurement of the effect of multiprogramming, and measurement of utilization and efficiency of program modules. A brief account of these problems is given below.

I. CPU utilization is frequently used as a measure of system throughput. However, such interpretation can be grossly misleading. It is necessary to distinguish between the CPU time used up by individual jobs and the CPU time used up by various supervisory functions (CPU scheduling, I/O scheduling, interrupt processing, memory management). That is, it is necessary to distinguish between the useful work and the system overhead. System overhead is a very important factor. In certain systems (e.g., paging systems) overhead may grow to an extent that no useful work is done (thrashing).

Utilization of a system or a system component is measured as the relative activity of the system or the component, that is, the ratio active (busy) time/total elapsed time. The active time can be broken down by operation types, job classes, or individual jobs. Such division generates a utilization profile. A CPU utilization profile is a source of information for analysis of the CPU overhead and for determining characteristics of the system workload.

II. Multiprogramming systems allow several independent jobs to compete for system resources (hardware and software components). Jobs with nonconflicting resource requirements can execute in parallel. Multiprogramming increases sytem throughput. On the other hand, a job may have to wait for various resources in the course of its execution. Waiting increases job turnaround time. The elapsed time multi-programming factor (ETMF) listed in Table 2.3 (performance measures) is one of the possible measures of the impact of multiprogramming. The relation between the response time of an interactive system and the number of simultaneous users is another measure of the multiprogramming effect. However, these measures do not identify the cause of job delays. To understand the effects of multiprogramming, it is necessary to measure the demands and the waiting times for individual system resources.

III. Some portions of a program are executed with much greater frequency than others and account for a major part of the total CPU time used by the program. Experience shows that about 80% of program execution time is spent in about 20% of the program code. If a computer system uses a hierarchy of memories of different speed, the most frequently used parts of a program should always be kept in the fastest memory, while the less frequently used parts can be stored in lower speed memories without noticeable performance degra-dation. Program efficiency can be increased by changes of algorithms or by improving the code. However, as in the case of memory allocation, it is first necessary to know what portions of a program consume most of the execution time, since only improvement in these areas can have a significant impact on the over-all execution time.

A.1 THE MEASURED SYSTEM

The hardware configuration of the measured system S is shown in figure A.1. All PMS level components operate asynchronously and they communicate with the CPU via interrupts. The software of the system S, as shown in figure A.2, is hierarchically structured. The level 0 is the system supervisor that controls two subsystems: the interactive system and the batch system The system S has the following characteristics:

I/O Devices

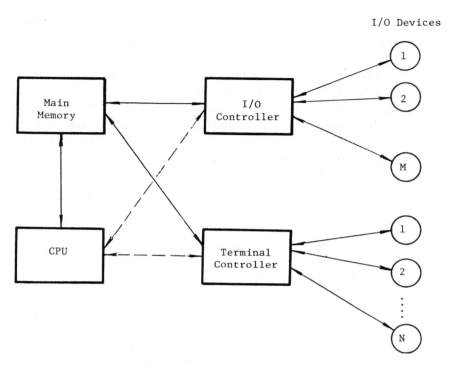

Figure A.1. Block diagram of the hardware configuration of the system *S*. Legend: ⟶, data; --►, control.

1. The batch system is multi-programmed between the quick batch and the standard batch. Batch jobs are identified as quick batch (**QB**) or standard batch (**SB**) jobs.
2. The interactive system supports *N* terminals. Each transaction between a user and the interactive system represents a job. These jobs are identified by the terminal number ($T1, T2, \ldots,$ TN).
3. Interrupts from PMS components are handled entirely by the system supervisor.

Finally, measurability of the system *S* can be described as follows:

1. Occurrence and duration of interrupts from individual PMS components is measurable with an ordinary hardware monitor.

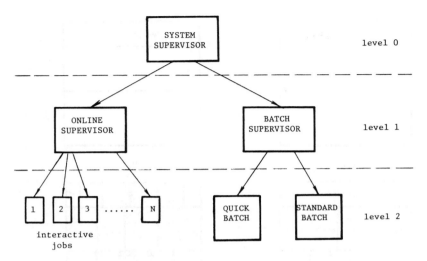

Figure A.2. Organization of the *OS* level of the system *S*.

2. The current level of execution (level 0, 1, 2) is measurable with an ordinary hardware monitor.
3. The system *S* supports a DCMI interface discussed in Section 6.7. The monitor interface consists of three M-registers, MRS, MRI, MRB, where MRS is under exclusive control of the system supervisor, MRI belongs to the interactive system, and MRB to the batch system.

A.2 CPU UTILIZATION PROFILE

Problem: Determine the profile of CPU utilization across individual software levels. Determine the profile of the CPU time charged to individual jobs.

Figure A.3 illustrates the total used CPU time as a block. This block is divided vertically, representing the distribution of the used CPU time among the individual levels, and horizontally, representing the distribution of the used CPU time among software components executing on the same level. Figures A.3(b) to A.3(d) show various profiles of CPU utilization for $N = 3$.

CPU utilization is measured most accurately with a hardware monitor, but it is impossible to relate measured utilization to running

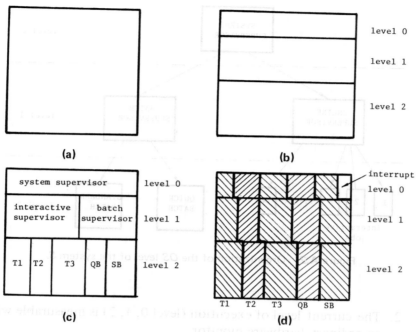

Figure A.3. CPU utilization profile. (a) Total CPU busy time; (b) The CPU utilization profile by levels; (c) The CPU utilization profile by levels and jobs; (d) The profile of time chargeable to individual jobs.

jobs and operations of the software system. A hardware monitor can measure the CPU utilization along the vertical line only (figure A.3b). CPU sharing along the horizontal line is not supported by any special hardware; a record about the inner state of each level is kept in the main memory and is thus concealed to a hardware monitor. The utilization profile along the horizontal line has to be measured by a hybrid method.

Solution: Each measured component (job or subsystem) is assigned one latch of the M-register of its immediate supervisor. The supervisor sets a specific latch just before control is passed to the associated component and resets the latch just after control is taken back from the component. The hardware monitor then measures duration of the activities described in Table A.1. The measured entities can be further combined, either directly by the processing element, or later during the interpretation phase. Such combinations are referred to as derived measures.

Table A.1
Measurement of the CPU Utilization Profile of System S

Composition of the system state vector ($N = 3$)

x_1	CPU busy
x_2	Interrupt
x_3	Level 0
x_4	Level 1
x_5	Level 2
x_6	Interactive system (MRS 1)
x_7	Batch system (MRS 2)
x_8	T1 (MRI 1)
x_9	T2 (MRI 2)
x_{10}	T3 (MRI 3)
x_{11}	QB (MRB 1)
x_{12}	SB (MRB 2)

where MRX n is the nth latch of the specified M-register.

Measured activities

	x_1	x_2	x_3	x_4	x_5	x_6	x_7	x_8	x_9	x_{10}	x_{11}	x_{12}	
a_1	0	0	0	0	0	0	0	0	0	0	0	0	CPU wait
a_2	1	1	1	0	0	d	d	d	d	d	d	d	CPU processing an interrupt
a_3	1	0	1	0	0	1	0	1	0	0	d	d	T1, level 0
a_4	1	0	1	0	0	1	0	0	1	0	d	d	T2, level 0
a_5	1	0	1	0	0	1	0	0	0	1	d	d	T3, level 0
a_6	1	0	1	0	0	0	1	d	d	d	1	0	QB, level 0
a_7	1	0	1	0	0	0	1	d	d	d	0	1	SB, level 0
a_8	1	0	0	1	0	1	0	1	0	0	d	d	T1, level 1
a_9	1	0	0	1	0	1	0	0	1	0	d	d	T2, level 1
a_{10}	1	0	0	1	0	1	0	0	0	1	d	d	T3, level 1
a_{11}	1	0	0	1	0	0	1	d	d	d	1	0	QB, level 1
a_{12}	1	0	0	1	0	0	1	d	d	d	0	1	SB, level 1
a_{13}	1	0	0	0	1	1	0	1	0	0	d	d	T1, level 2
a_{14}	1	0	0	0	1	1	0	0	1	0	d	d	T2, level 2
a_{15}	1	0	0	0	1	1	0	0	0	1	d	d	T3, level 2
a_{16}	1	0	0	0	1	0	1	d	d	d	1	0	QB, level 2
a_{17}	1	0	0	0	1	0	1	d	d	d	0	1	SB, level 2

where d is 'don't care' state

Derived measures

$a_2 + a_3 + a_4 + a_5 + a_6 + a_7$	System supervisor
$a_8 + a_9 + a_{10}$	Interactive supervisor
$a_{11} + a_{12}$	Batch supervisor
$a_{13} + a_{14} + a_{15}$	Interactive problem programs
$a_{16} + a_{17}$	Batch problem program
$a_3 + a_8 + a_{13}$	T1
$a_4 + a_9 + a_{14}$	T2
$a_5 + a_{10} + a_{15}$	T3
$a_6 + a_{11} + a_{16}$	QB
$a_7 + a_{12} + a_{17}$	SB

One problem that remains to be solved is concerned with accounting for the CPU time required to handle interrupts unrelated to the currently executing jobs. In the scheme presented here, this time is not explicitly chargeable to any job. However, it is possible to determine the cost of processing a single interrupt and add it to the cost of an operation that generated the interrupt (e.g., disk I/O).

The described instrumentation facilitates measurement of the time chargeable to individual subsystems:

1. A specific terminal
2. A specific batch partition

Since each of these subsystems can be used by many different users (on a time-shared basis, of course), further measurements are necessary to determine resource requirements of individual users. The record of which users are using the system at any moment is maintained by the system. This record can be combined with the outcome of the described measurements to produce the desired information.

A.3 MULTIPROGRAMMING EFFECTS

Problem: Analyze the multiprogramming effects in the interactive system.

Each job competes for system resources with other jobs currently in the system. The state of a job is defined with respect to system resources. Let k be the number of possible states of an interactive job. Figure A.4 is a state diagram for interactive jobs running on the system S, where $k = 5$. At first, a job has to be assigned main memory. Then, if the CPU is free, this job can begin its execution; otherwise, it has to wait. Once assigned the CPU, a job may execute until it:

1. Runs out of the allocated time
2. Issues a request for additional memory
3. Issues an I/O request

The problem calls for measurement of the time spent in each individual state as a function of the number of active terminals.

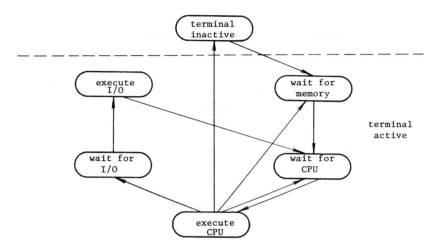

Figure A.4. State diagram of an interactive job.

Solution: Each terminal is assigned $k + 1$ latches of the MRI. These latches are set and cleared by the supervisor of the interactive system. The instrumentation and measurements for $N = 3$ are described in Table A.2.

The given equations describe only a subset of activities that can be measured with this particular instrumentation. Other possible measurements are the number of jobs waiting for each of the resources. Also, it is possible to obtain an execution profile for different user commands by keeping a parallel record of commands issued from a specific terminal. Unfortunately, the hybrid approach gets out of hand if the number of terminals in the system is large, which is a more typical case than the simple example discussed here, and it becomes necessary to use an internal trace monitor.

A.4 SOFTWARE UTILIZATION AND EFFICIENCY

Problem: Determine the use and the efficiency of the programs that compose the system supervisor.

A number of methods for measuring program efficiency have been proposed and implemented [DARD70, ESTR67B, HOLW71, NEME71, ROEK69, RUDD72, SAAL72, STUC72]. Hardware moni-

Table A.2
Measurement of the Effect of Multiprogramming in System S

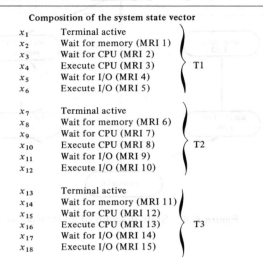

Composition of the system state vector

x_1	Terminal active	
x_2	Wait for memory (MRI 1)	
x_3	Wait for CPU (MRI 2)	
x_4	Execute CPU (MRI 3)	T1
x_5	Wait for I/O (MRI 4)	
x_6	Execute I/O (MRI 5)	
x_7	Terminal active	
x_8	Wait for memory (MRI 6)	
x_9	Wait for CPU (MRI 7)	
x_{10}	Execute CPU (MRI 8)	T2
x_{11}	Wait for I/O (MRI 9)	
x_{12}	Execute I/O (MRI 10)	
x_{13}	Terminal active	
x_{14}	Wait for memory (MRI 11)	
x_{15}	Wait for CPU (MRI 12)	
x_{16}	Execute CPU (MRI 13)	T3
x_{17}	Wait for I/O (MRI 14)	
x_{18}	Execute I/O (MRI 15)	

Measured activities

	x_1	x_2	x_3	x_4	x_5	x_6	x_7	x_8	x_9	x_{10}	x_{11}	x_{12}	x_{13}	x_{14}	x_{15}	x_{16}	x_{17}	x_{18}	
a_1	0	d	d	d	d	d	d	d	d	d	d	d	d	d	d	d	d	d	Terminal 1 inactive
a_2	d	d	d	d	d	d	0	d	d	d	d	d	d	d	d	d	d	d	Terminal 2 inactive
a_3	d	d	d	d	d	d	d	d	d	d	d	d	0	d	d	d	d	d	Terminal 3 inactive
a_4	1	1	0	0	0	0	d	d	d	d	d	d	d	d	d	d	d	d	T1 waiting for memory
a_5	1	0	1	0	0	0	d	d	d	d	d	d	d	d	d	d	d	d	T1 waiting for CPU
a_6	1	0	0	1	0	0	d	d	d	0	d	d	d	d	d	0	d	d	T1 has CPU
a_7	1	0	0	0	1	0	d	d	d	d	d	d	d	d	d	d	d	d	T1 waiting for I/O
a_8	1	0	0	0	0	1	d	d	d	d	d	d	d	d	d	d	d	d	T1 doing I/O
a_9	d	d	d	d	d	d	1	1	0	0	0	0	d	d	d	d	d	d	T2 waiting for memory
a_{10}	d	d	d	d	d	d	1	0	1	0	0	0	d	d	d	d	d	d	T2 waiting for CPU
a_{11}	d	d	d	0	d	d	1	0	0	1	0	0	d	d	d	0	d	d	T2 has CPU
a_{12}	d	d	d	d	d	d	1	0	0	0	1	0	d	d	d	d	d	d	T2 waiting for I/O
a_{13}	d	d	d	d	d	d	1	0	0	0	0	1	d	d	d	d	d	d	T2 doing I/O
a_{14}	d	d	d	d	d	d	d	d	d	d	d	d	1	1	0	0	0	0	T3 waiting for memory
a_{15}	d	d	d	d	d	d	d	d	d	d	d	d	1	0	1	0	0	0	T3 waiting for CPU
a_{16}	d	d	d	0	d	d	d	d	d	0	d	d	1	0	0	1	0	0	T3 has CPU
a_{17}	d	d	d	d	d	d	d	d	d	d	d	d	1	0	0	0	1	0	T3 waiting for I/O
a_{18}	d	d	d	d	d	d	d	d	d	d	d	d	1	0	0	0	0	1	T3 doing I/O

where d is 'don't care' state

Continued

$a_i \cdot a_2 \cdot a_3$		Time T1 spends in state i when no other terminal is active
$a_i \cdot (a_2 \oplus a_3)$	$i = 4, 5, 6, 7, 8$	Time T1 spends in state i when two terminals are active
$a_i \cdot \bar{a}_2 \cdot \bar{a}_3$		Time T1 spends in state i when three terminals are active
$a_j \cdot a_1 \cdot a_3$		Time T2 spends in state j when no other terminal is active
$a_j \cdot (a_1 \oplus a_3)$	$j = 9, 10, 11, 12, 13$	Time T2 spends in state j when two terminals are active
$a_j \cdot \bar{a}_1 \cdot \bar{a}_3$		Time T2 spends in state j when three terminals are active
$a_k \cdot a_1 \cdot a_2$		Time T3 spends in state k when no other terminal is active
$a_k \cdot (a_1 \oplus a_2)$	$k = 14, 15, 16, 17, 18$	Time T3 spends in state k when two terminals are active
$a_k \cdot \bar{a}_1 \cdot \bar{a}_2$		Time T3 spends in state k when three terminals are active

Derived measures

$a_4 \cdot (a_2 \oplus a_3) + a_9 \cdot (a_1 \oplus a_3) + a_{14} \cdot (a_1 \oplus a_2)$	Wait for memory when two terminals are active
$a_4 \cdot \bar{a}_2 \cdot \bar{a}_3 + a_9 \cdot \bar{a}_1 \cdot \bar{a}_3 + a_{14} \cdot \bar{a}_1 \cdot \bar{a}_2$	Wait for memory when three terminals are active
$a_5 \cdot (a_2 \oplus a_3) + a_{10} \cdot (a_1 \oplus a_3) + a_{15} \cdot (a_1 \oplus a_2)$	Wait for CPU when two terminals are active
$a_5 \cdot \bar{a}_2 \cdot \bar{a}_3 + a_{10} \cdot \bar{a}_1 \cdot \bar{a}_3 + a_{15} \cdot \bar{a}_1 \cdot \bar{a}_2$	Wait for CPU when three terminals are active
$a_7 \cdot (a_2 \oplus a_3) + a_{12} \cdot (a_1 \oplus a_3) + a_{17} \cdot (a_1 \oplus a_2)$	Wait for I/O when two terminals are active
$a_7 \cdot \bar{a}_2 \cdot \bar{a}_3 + a_{12} \cdot \bar{a}_1 \cdot \bar{a}_3 + a_{17} \cdot \bar{a}_1 \cdot \bar{a}_2$	Wait for I/O when three terminals are active

tors can measure time spent in individual program sections by recording addresses of executed instructions. It is, of course, necessary to know how the measured program is mapped during its execution into the address space measurable by a hardware monitor. This mapping must not change during program's execution. An internal software monitor can measure time intervals either by sampling or directly. A sampling monitor periodically interrupts the measured program and records the address of the current instruction. Again, it is necessary to know what that address corresponds to in the program source code. Accuracy of the sampling technique is a function of the number of samples collected at random during the measurement period. The shorter the measured time interval, the higher sampling rate is necessary. Sampling overhead may become intolerably high as the sampling rate increases. Furthermore, software sampling cannot be used to time those system routines that are not interruptible by the timer routine. This may lead to a significant measurement error, as was demonstrated in a study by Peterson [PETE74].

The direct timing method consists of reading the system clock at the beginning and the end of a program section and calculating the difference. Process preemption and interrupts may temporarily suspend the measured activity; the clock that measures duration of this activity must then be stopped, too. Such a facility, known as virtual clock, is provided by some operating systems. If the system does not provide a virtual clock, it is possible to use a real time clock (time-of-day clock), that is independent of what the system does. However, if an interrupt or a preemption occurs during a measurement, this measurement is completely invalidated. Hybrid monitoring can eliminate this problem. The hybrid method is flexible and efficient, especially when measuring deeply nested routines.

Rather than working with program modules or routines, a logical block of code is chosen as an entity for instrumentation; such a scheme is a convenient means for changing the level of detail in a measurement.

Consider a set of blocks $B = B_i$, $i = 1,2, \ldots , n$, with a relation @ between blocks of a set B, where @ has the following properties:

(1) TRANSITIVE: If B_i @ B_j and B_j @ B_k, then B_i @ B_k
(2) ASYMMETRIC: If B_i @ B_j, then B_j $\cancel{@}$ B_i
(3) REFLEXIVE: B_i @ B_i

where B_i @ B_j means that B_j is logically nested in B_i. The block B_j is

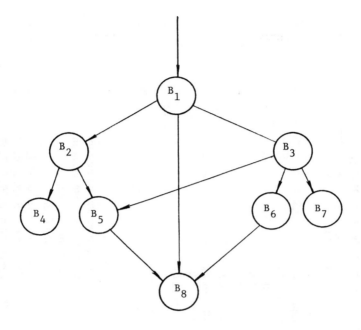

$B_i \ @ \ B_j$

Figure A.5. Set of monitored program blocks and their relation.

called the nested block; B_i is the nesting block. The third property, reflexivity, allows recursive routines. Figure A.5 illustrates a set B of size 8 with the relation @. The connections in this diagram represent @, with the arrow pointing to the nested block.

The measurement problem can be restated as follows:

1. How frequently is each B_i executed and what percentage of the total CPU time is spent in B_i?
2. For each pair B_i, B_j such that $B_i \ @ \ B_j$, how frequently is B_j entered from B_i and what percentage of the total[1] B_i execution time is spent in B_j?

---

[1] Total execution time of B_i includes time spent in routines called by B_i.

Table A.3
Measurement of Utilization and Efficiency of Supervisory Programs in System S

Composition of the system state vector

x_1	CPU busy
x_2	Interrupt
x_3	Execution of B_1
x_4	Execution of B_2
x_5	Execution of B_3
x_6	Execution of B_4
x_7	Execution of B_5
x_8	Execution of B_6
x_9	Execution of B_7
x_{10}	Execution of B_8

Measured activities

	x_1	x_2	x_3	x_4	x_5	x_6	x_7	x_8	x_9	x_{10}	
a_1	0	0	d	d	d	d	d	d	d	d	CPU wait
a_2	1	1	d	d	d	d	d	d	d	d	CPU processing an interrupt
a_3	1	0	0	0	0	0	0	0	0	0	CPU busy, not executing any of the monitored blocks
a_4	1	0	1	0	0	0	0	0	0	0	Execution of B_1
a_5	1	0	1	1	0	0	0	0	0	0	Execution of $B_2(B_1 @ B_2)$
a_6	1	0	1	0	1	0	0	0	0	0	Execution of $B_3(B_1 @ B_3)$
a_7	1	0	1	1	0	1	0	0	0	0	Execution of $B_4(B_1 @ B_2 @ B_4)$
a_8	1	0	1	1	0	0	1	0	0	0	Execution of $B_5(B_1 @ B_2 @ B_5)$
a_9	1	0	1	0	1	0	1	0	0	0	Execution of $B_5(B_1 @ B_3 @ B_5)$

	Execution of $B_6(B_1 @ B_3 @ B_6)$	Execution of $B_7(B_1 @ B_3 @ B_7)$	Execution of $B_8(B_1 @ B_2 @ B_5 @ B_8)$	Execution of $B_8(B_1 @ B_3 @ B_5 @ B_8)$	Execution of $B_8(B_1 @ B_8)$
a_{10}	1	0	0	0	0
a_{11}	1	0	0	1	0
a_{12}	1	0	1	0	1
a_{13}	1	0	0	1	0
a_{14}	1	0	0	0	1

where d is 'don't care' state

Derived measures

Execution of B_5	$a_8 + a_9$
Total execution time of B_1	$a_4 + a_5 + a_6 + a_7 + a_8 + a_9 + a_{10} + a_{11} + a_{12} + a_{13} + a_{14}$
Total execution time of B_2	$a_5 + a_7 + a_8 + a_{12}$
Total execution time of B_3	$a_6 + a_9 + a_{10} + a_{11} + a_{13}$
Total execution time of B_5	$a_8 + a_9 + a_{12} + a_{13}$
Total execution time of B_8	$a_{12} + a_{13} + a_{14}$

The second part can be accomplished only with a monitor that is capable of identifying the nesting block B_i. A hybrid monitor is the most efficient tool for this type of measurement.

Solution: Assign each block B_i one latch of the MRS. Every time a block B_i is entered, it sets its latch and clears it upon exit. CPU time spent handling interrupts can be measured (and discounted) by monitoring the interrupt latches set by the system hardware. The instrumentation and measurements for the set B shown in figure A.5 are described in Table A.3.

To measure how the system supervisory software is used by individual subsystems, this experiment can be combined with the experiment described in Section A.2. The system state vector then includes also the elements x_6 to x_{12} from Section A.2.

With the monitoring facilities available in the system, it is also possible to measure efficiency of the components of the online supervisor (using MRO) or the batch supervisor (using MRB). Programs running on level 2 have no access to the monitor interface. However, since individual user programs do not affect the efficiency of the over-all system and operate in an interruptible mode, a sampling technique usually provides sufficiently accurate statistics. Special software tools capable of monitoring an arbitrary problem program are available. These monitors execute as an ordinary job. They load the monitored program and supervise its execution; the monitored program is interrupted at regular intervals such that the monitor can record the location of the current instruction [HOLW71, JOHN71].

The problems discussed in this Appendix were encountered in the course of evaluating performance of the administrative information system at Stanford University. The fundamental performance measures of this system, the throughput and the response time, or *how* the system performs, were measured with a software monitor. Succeeding hybrid measurements were then directed toward understanding *why* the system performs the way it does. These measurement experiments were described in [SVOB73A, SVOB73B].

BIBLIOGRAPHY

Entries marked with an asterisk (*) are referenced in the text.

*DARD70   Darden, S.C., Heller, S.B., "Streamline Your Software Development", *Computer Decisions,* Vol. 2, No. 10, October 1970, pp. 29–33.

*ESTR67B   Estrin, G., Hopkins, D., Coggan, B., Crocker, S.D., "SNUPER Computer—A Computer in Instrumentation Automation", *AFIPS Proc. SJCC,* Thompson Books, Washington, D.C., 1967, pp. 645–656.

*HOLW71   Holtwick, G.M., "Designing a Commercial Performance Measurement System", *Proc. ACM SIGOPS Workshop on System Performance Evaluation,* April 1971, pp. 29–58.

*NEME71   Nemeth, A.G., Rovner, P.D., "User Program Measurement in a Time-Shared Environment", *Communications of the ACM,* Vol. 14, No. 10, October 1971, pp. 661–666.

*PETE74   Peterson, T.G., "A Comparsion of Software and Hardware Monitors", *ACM Performance Evaluation Review,* Vol. 3, No. 3, September 1973, pp. 2–5.

*ROEK69   Roek, D.J., Emerson, W.C., "A Hardware Instrumentation Approach to Evaluation of a Large Scale System", *Proc. 24th ACM National Conference,* 1969, pp. 351–367.

*RUUD72   Ruud, R.J., "The CPM-X—A System Approach to Performance Measurement", *AFIPS Proc. FJCC,* 1972, pp. 949–951.

*SAAL72   Saal, H.J., Shustek, L.J., "Microprogrammed Implementation of Computer Measurement Techniques", *Proc. ACM 5th Annual Workshop on Microprogramming,* September 1972, pp. 42–50.

*STUC72   Stucki, L.G., "A Prototype Automatic Program Testing Tool", *AFIPS Proc. FJCC,* 1972, pp. 829–836.

*SVOB73A   Svobodova, L., "Online System Performance Measurements with Software and Hybrid Monitors", *Proc. ACM SIGOPS Fourth Symposium on Operating System Principles,* October 1973, pp. 45–53.

*SVOB73B   Svobodova, L., "Measuring Computer System Utilization with a Hardware and a Hybrid Monitor", *ACM SICME Performance Evaluation Review,* No. 4, 1973, pp. 20–34.

Index